MW00813733

ARTISTRY

Pursuing the Mysteries of Music Performance

ROBERT W. DEMAREE
Indiana University South Bend

ROBERT HAMILTON
Arizona State University Tempe

ARTS HERITAGE
Chandler

Copyright 2021 Arts Heritage

All rights reserved, including the right of
reproduction in whole or in part in any form.

Arts Heritage and its colophon are trademarks
of Arts Heritage, LLC.
4214 West Dublin Court
Chandler, AZ 85226

ISBN: 978-1-7923-1157-4

Library of Congress Control Number: 2020915994

The cover design is based upon a photograph of pianist Sidney Foster,
courtesy of Justin Foster

Editor: Jeanne Martin Dams
Typesetting: Soundview Design
Printer: Sheridan Books, Inc.

Contents

Foreword

Anthony Newman

This is a unique and completely original book about the performance of classical music. Along with the text discussion it offers freshly recorded interpretations of famous piano works, performed to suggest various artistic possibilities. Generally small sections are utilized, demonstrating the importance of interpretive freedom in the performance of musical compositions.

In general, the earlier a composition was written, the more was added [by the performer] to its performance in terms of notes, words, or even time freedoms. There are many masses from the fifteenth century that specify the part of the mass, for example *Kyrie*, and provide only notes, to which performers must add the text freely and at their own discretion. This is also true in the later Baroque with respect to the additions of ornaments. Indeed, there are preludes from the early to middle 1600s for harpsichord, especially those of Louis Couperin, that give us bare notes only and some slurs, to which we add the note values (i.e. sixteenths, eighths, and quarter notes). Music seems to stop allowing freedom of addition sometime around 1850, perhaps earlier in the case of certain composers, such as Beethoven in his late works, and most of the piano music of Chopin. There are, however, quite a few examples of Chopin embellishing his own texts.

In the case of continuo—filling out the left hand with

chords, for example—we know that Schumann himself added piano continuo to his symphonies when they were performed. Continuo, probably invented in Venice, Italy in the mid-1600s, made it easier for a composer simply to write numbers for the chords that the accompanist would play in an orchestral piece, instead of laboriously writing them out. This tradition continues all the way through to about 1830, but varies from national style to national style. The last spectacular example I know of is in Beethoven's "Emperor" Concerto, finally published by Bärenreiter with the composer's continuo additions. I have never heard anyone play this great work with these additions by the composer.

In this excellent study, the addition of notes to original music is revealed with wonderful improvisatory freedom in the Bartók audio examples.

Here is a list of what was "flexible" in the performance of music, shall we say up to the mature period of Brahms, circa 1850:

1. The free addition of cadenzas or flourishes at places in a composition marked with the word 'cadenza', or the sign for fermata. These flourishes or cadenzas were added in vocal music certainly from 1600, all the way through the fourth concerto of Beethoven, including all the concerti of Mozart and Bach.

2. The free addition of ornaments in French music until the revolution in 1790, and in German music probably until 1820. There are many treatises that tell us the style of the ornamentation and how it was performed.

3. Changing duplets into triplets and the reverse, especially in jigs.

4. Over dotting; that is, playing the note or notes following a dot later than notated. This technique was completely documented in the 1690s by a Frenchman named Loulié.

5. Bunching notes together, for example in fast compositions where groups of note values are slurred (or not), and where fingering makes it almost impossible to play as written. One bunches, for example, four notes into the time of three notes. The earliest discussion I know of this is in Quantz, and the latest in a letter of Beethoven to Czerny discussing a new piano student's performance of these kinds of passages.

6. Playing groups of notes unequally, as is done in jazz today. This was known as *notes inégales* in French music, and probably was utilized in German and Italian music that had characteristically French influences. This ended with the French Revolution, when most French composers fled France—often to London, to start what would be known as the French romantic period.

7. Using an interesting *rubato* called a "fringe" in England and "suspension" in French music, especially that of François Couperin. In these examples, even though both hands are written together, the left-hand plays its note just slightly before the right hand.

8. Pointing out beat alterations, i.e., changing groups of 4/4 into those of 3/4 or 3/2, by making the accents conform to the changed bars.

9. Accenting words in a song or accenting them in the performance of the same song in, for example, a transcription of it for solo piano.

10. The shortening of note values on what were called 'weak beats' in the Baroque and classical periods, but not in the romantic.

Certainly, one of the most important areas addressed in this book is how music is performed with time flexibility by seasoned artists, a technique which cannot really be taught but perhaps can be imitated. It is especially prevalent in great artists whose performances touch one!

Artistry focuses on the importance of freedom in interpretation, revealed in the text and audio demonstrations through works of great composers who are insightfully penned in their historical contexts. I hope the authors will create more books about this important area, utilizing standard works. There should be more books like this.

Anthony Newman

Preface

It is greatly significant to the authors that a distinguished scholar has shared his thoughts on the subject of this study. Leading scholar-performer Anthony Newman, who transformed Baroque performance practices of a generation of eminent musicians, has enriched our efforts with his contributions, and we extend to him our deep gratitude.

Over several years we have sought the advice of another remarkable source: some of our readers may not realize that Paul Aurandt—well known as the writer Paul Harvey, Jr.—is also a professional pianist and composer. His successes at the Chicago Musical College and since have made him our perfect consultant for this effort, and we thank him gratefully for that, and for his important encouragement.

Many colleagues and students—far too many to mention individually—have contributed ideas and reflections to one or both of us. We are thankful for the technical support of Kuang-Li Huang and Charles Szczepanek in the recording of the performance examples, as well as to Yuriy Vereshchagin for his computer backup. Gregory Hamilton has been generous with his time and valued assistance, and we also thank Bryn Cannon, James Foy Cebastien, Moye Chen, Robert K. Demaree, Justin Foster, Kate Hamilton, Victoria Shively, and Xiaoyu Zheng for their important contributions. Most of all, we are indebted to our superb editor, Jeanne M. Dams.

List of Illustrations

List of Musical Examples

A Tribute

Robert William Demaree, Jr. (1937-2020)

I believe it was sometime in 2012 that Robert Demaree approached me about writing this book together—one in which we would not only explore artistic freedom, but also provide recorded excerpts as examples. The idea was exciting, and I felt honored to be asked to team up with a close friend and colleague who had already co-authored several highly respected textbooks, including *The Masses of Joseph Haydn* (first comprehensive study of Haydn's Masses since 1940, and the first ever to be published in English).

From the outset Bob and I intended to dedicate this volume to our mothers, Helen and Winona, and also to our wives, Beverley and Lynn, who have had an extraordinary influence on our lives, both personal and professional. That dedication remains. What we did not anticipate is that before these words found publication, one of the two of us would no longer be here on Earth.

And so, with great respect and fond gratitude, I wish to pay homage to my remarkable co-author, Robert W. Demaree. I am grateful to have shared a part of this world with him. And now you will as well.

Robert Hamilton

Introduction

In this book we offer our view of means by which the performance of music can approach the lofty dimensions of the masters' creations themselves: hence Artistry. It is our contention that producing inspired performances requires a *search*, which, while it fully respects, embraces, and absorbs the notated score, also probes, intuits, and experiments in pursuit of the music's intentions—wherever the search may lead and to whatever extent is possible. In so doing, we ought to awaken the creative freedom the great composers themselves have employed while performing their composed and scored works.

Van Cliburn said it: "Music is God's language." Surely there can be no questioning its uniqueness, or its ability to excite, penetrate, and renew us. There is no other language like it.

PART I

Words and Music

CHAPTER ONE
Artistry and Interpretation

Demaree & Hamilton

In today's competitive world of music performance, we can probably agree that all who succeed in entering it are diligent, and that all share certain physical gifts. Yet some of these individuals may never be justifiably described as "Artists."

Why are the very finest performing musicians commonly called **Artists**[1], after all? What attributes identify them? What sets them apart?

The definitive answer is: They are those who have artistic insights above the commonplace. We suggest that such "artistic insights above the commonplace" cannot be identified as deft replicas of a composer's unique intention, but that performers should be coolly encouraged to interpret (supplement) the score.

Then what of a common assumption that each work bears in it a singular **interpretation** —the composer's very own intent? Is there any way we can know if the composer

---

1   Please note: When a salient word first occurs in a given chapter, it will appear in bold type and will be listed in the Glossary, pages 187-190.

had one specific realization in mind, and, if so, what it was? Some may hope to resolve such questions through reading witnessed reports of past composers' own performances (or by hearing recordings of the more recent ones). Others believe the answer is, simply, the score itself, while still others might look to what is known about the nature of a given composer's compositional process. Beethoven, we know, was especially meticulous about what he finally submitted to paper; we discover this in his sketchbooks. [EN 1-1] Bartók even noted the number of minutes and seconds some of his pieces should require in performance. [EN 1-2] Nevertheless, neither seems to have strictly followed his own score indications in performance. And Chopin was known to play his pieces in ways that strayed far from his written directions. [EN 1-3] (A more extensive discussion of the performance practices of composers will be found in Chapter 11, Stage and Studio: Composers and Performing.)

How does a workmanlike musician become an Artist, whose performances reveal music's loftiest dimensions? What should be the principal goals? Consider: While essential, the music score is only a map or printed plan. Each individual journey must be ours as performers. What is implied, for example, when the composer writes *forte*? Or *allegro, crescendo, ritardando,* for that matter? We get the general idea, of course, but how loud should a given *forte* be, and how fast an *allegro*?

This consideration parallels another of the performed arts, theatre. A playwright's script is much like a composer's score: it provides the essential matter for the actors, together with, perhaps, some advice about the presentation of that material. It does *not*, however, deny the actors latitude in their individualized performances.[2]

Another non-musical analogy: Some biblical scriptures are linked to specific dates in the church year and are used by clerics the world over, each directing remarks (as a sermon or homily) in an explanatory way to a local congregation. These clergy select a designated scripture as theme for the sermon—that is, as a "text." Thousands may preach on the same text, while varying their words and conclusions as seems best for their congregations at that moment in history.[3]

Each of these parallel circumstances—the musician's performance of a score, the actor's delivery of the lines of a script, and the cleric's amplification of a scriptural text—is an interpretation, and the composer, the playwright, and the bishop will each expect freedom on the part of the "performer"—the musician, actor, or cleric. The delivered script and sermon must encourage us to examine our minds and consciences, and so must revelations of the composer's score (which, since it does not depend on verbiage, can be particularly opaque with respect to performance). In the view of the present authors, a

---

2   It is worth noting that general societal preferences have often influenced interpretive practices over the centuries. For example, consider young Prince Hamlet's angry confrontation with his mother, Queen Gertrude, in her bedroom. [EN 1-4] Between the premiere of *Hamlet* and Sigmund Freud's positing of an *Oedipal complex*, three centuries elapsed. Presentations of Shakespeare's play during that span of time seem to have explained Hamlet's anger by citing what the young prince calls "my virtue". But once Freud had claimed a broad base for his theory it became trendy, and soon stage and film productions of the play used explicit sexual suggestion to explain Hamlet's anger.

3   The intent of the message may vary self-indulgently: the German Army traveled along roads into battle in World War I employing as a marching song Martin Luther's "*Ein feste Burg ist unser Gott.*"

principal stumbling block to **Artistry** in music performance is the exclusive focus on score markings, never fully consulting our personal **intuitions.** A work conceived in this manner will not likely unfold or develop very much during one's life with the piece.

Over the years, author/pianist Hamilton has worked with as many as twenty composers in preparation for performances of their music. While he remembers being asked to be freer in expressing his own ideas, he does not recall any requests to follow the score markings more faithfully. And why should this be surprising? Composers, like the general public, will certainly prefer performances of their works that are original and convincing over those which are superficially "correct."

Cannot both preferences—the composer's and the performer's—be satisfied (merge) in a given performance? Yes, of course they can. It is even likely that the thoughts and sensations from which an Artist performer completes the creative process will closely resemble that which began in the composer's own imagination. But again, the haunting question for many conscientious performers is this: Did the composer have a specific intention in mind, and if so, what was it?

Common Impediments to Performance Artistry

Some basic performance shortcomings are widespread. One performer might be too rigidly metronomic, while another may make excessive use of *rubato* (even to the point of dismantling important rhythmic relationships). Yet others overstate things, losing subtle nuances in the process. In some performances melodic lines are overwhelmed by the accompaniment, leaving the music with no clear line of leadership. And many performers will focus so much on physical skills that their technical potency literally leaves the music itself behind, often producing fireworks which are not integrated with the artistic context of the work.

Consider for a moment that human beings commonly seek superlatives. We contest each other. We award prizes to those who can run or swim fastest, leap highest, lift the most. Other members of the animal kingdom use their speed for practical purposes—catching prey, eluding predators—but humans hold Olympic Games and the like.

For half of the twentieth century there was a world-wide fascination with the possibility of the four-minute mile. Could the human body actually perform at that rate? Then in 1954 Roger Bannister barely reached that goal for the first known time, garnering international fame. Yet just a half-century later, runners were routinely matching his time, and winners were improving it by as much as a quarter of a minute!

A year earlier Hillary and Norgay had reached the peak of Mount Everest. Their unprecedented climb became a sensation. But by the early twenty-first century, "summiting Everest" had become so routine that climbers were complaining about the accumulation of trash and garbage left by previous expeditions. EN 1-5 The race, the climb—such ephemeral goals![4]

---

4 The great Mallory, who died on the highest stage of Everest in the 1930s (lacking the benefits of all the specialized equipment that would be developed in the coming decades), when asked his reason for climbing such a mountain, replied laconically, "Because it's there."

Humans thus set more-or-less irrelevant objectives for themselves, and may eventually achieve them, calling such accomplishments "a great victory for the Human Spirit," or something similar (even when the achievement may be little more than the triumph of a child who causes a stone to skip one extra time on a lake surface before it sinks). In like fashion, some musicians strive to play challenging passages faster than others have, as if faster was somehow better in the creative world of Art. But, to the contrary, "faster" often leads to shapeless and mechanical music performances. EN 1-6

Poorly shaped music also results when a relentless verticality—beat by beat and bar by bar—dominates. Such performances trudge through passages without direction or vision, failing to let the music breathe. Contrasts are either missing or crudely over-emphasized, and there will likely be little sense of the overall shape of the work.

An analogy can be found in the modern city-scape. When Louis Sullivan and others envisioned the upward thrust of the early skyscrapers, they were continuing an aesthetic that extended back past the towers of Gothic cathedrals to Babel itself. But the Chrysler and Empire State Buildings became iconic, so much so that city centers began to be peppered with tall structures less original and less evocative. Current tourists often cannot glimpse the tallest skyscrapers until they stand next to them. Intended—like the Gothic cathedral towers—as structural exclamation points, they must contrast with their surroundings. (Too many vertical exclamation points are monotonous and destroy shape!!!!!) Today, architects who want their buildings to have impact must look to other parameters.[5]

Some performers do not balance the intellectual and emotional aspects of music very well, often leaning excessively to the emotional side. The iconic, creative E.T.A. Hoffman—a member of the emotionally expressive Romantic school, no less—is surprisingly known to have warned that music must always be understood as intellectually grounded, not simply thought of as emotional in character. [EN 1-7] Of course there are those who go to the opposite extreme, carefully revealing architectural and intellectual properties but avoiding the music's emotional content. Sometimes this intellectual/emotional imbalance reflects a one-sided personality. But it can also result from shallow preparation, including insufficient study of the composer or of the work's construction.

Potential Impediments for even the Seasoned Professional

The comprehensive and uncorrupted performance of composed music relies on a sustained connection with the composer.

---

5 Disrupting exclamation points were also encountered in mid-twentieth century recorded music produced on 78-rpm discs called records. This worked well for most of the market (e.g. "pop" songs), but longer classical works, especially symphonies and operas, had to be spread over multiple discs. Record-players of the time were equipped with record-changers—devices that would automatically drop the next disc with a thud onto the previous one, and then move the needle-arm back into place. All this took some time, interrupting the flow of the music, but it was the only way to record major works. (The eventual move to LP, or "Long Playing" records afforded fewer interruptions.) One of the present authors still occasionally experiences this disorientation while listening, thanks to the 78-rpm recordings of Rachmaninoff and Tchaikovsky symphonies he repeatedly heard as a child. It is noteworthy that standard repeats were often eliminated—not because of performers' wishes, but to reduce the number of interruptions.

Performers of all levels impede Artistry when they seek stand-alone attention for themselves. At such moments audience concentration invariably shifts away from the music to the skills of the performer. One such disruption, introduced above, stems from the effort to play faster than others. Many exciting *sonata* and *concerto* finales containing grand, powerful potency when locked into a controlled tempo can, if performers wish to show off their speed, descend to disconnected races for the finish line. EN 1-8 Listeners lose their deeper involvement with the music, sit back, and simply "watch the show." If the performer makes it to the end unscathed, the crowd will predictably stand and cheer. But their enthusiasm will not emanate so much from true engagement with the music as from witnessing a self-obsessed exhibition of athletic technical skill.[6]

The temptation for performers to harvest self-recognition absent the composer is also present during slow, lyrical pieces. In this case it is slowness and *rubato* that may become obsessive, along with an exaggeration of dynamic nuance until the genuine character of the composition becomes distorted and trite. Such performing could be termed "gilding the lily," or applying unwanted embellishment to music that is more profoundly beautiful when left in its natural state of simplicity.

Undeniably there has always been some affectation—in certain periods, a considerable amount of chicanery—in music performance. Frequent, ostentatious clearings of the spitvalve by brass concerto soloists during orchestral *tutti* passages come to mind, as well as over-the-top physical movements unleashed by some string

---

6   It is also worth noting that a piece of music loses much of its essential *rhythmic energy* when the performance surpasses a given speed with consequent weakened pulse, no matter who the virtuoso may be.

soloists. Planned, often customary pauses for post-aria audience applause in operas (which may, with a star singer, grow to minutes-in-duration) unavoidably interrupt the shape and flow of the scene.

Visual displays of potentially distracting mannerisms have also come from conductors, in the years since ensemble growth and architectural change made these individuals performers, rather than standing spectators. [EN 1-9] Even the great, legendary Leonard Bernstein was known to sometimes thrash about on the podium—perhaps wishing to choreograph the music and bring greater understanding to his players and audience, or, perhaps, to draw more attention to himself. [EN 1-10] Author Demaree recalls that he watched the celebrated Eugene Ormandy use one set of straight-forward, simple, and completely effective gestures in rehearsal with the Philadelphia Orchestra in a Tchaikovsky symphony (for the players a familiar work, of course), but more florid and exaggerated motions during the concert that night. [EN 1-11]

There have been exaggerated theatrics from pianists of every generation, including our own. These include excessively throwing the arms around, stomping on the floor or damper pedal, and staging stereotyped, melodramatic facial gimmicks.

Besides causing distraction, a potential negative result from such practices is loss of acoustic focus and precision. It must never be forgotten that music is fundamentally an aural experience. That having been said, some visual enhancement in live performing can, when sincerely rooted in the music itself, provide added meaning and excitement for many listeners.[7]

---

7 It should also be noted that some of the most expressive interpreting has come from performers who offer very little, or no visual elaboration onstage. Legendary examples include the violinist Jascha Heifetz, pianist Sviatoslav Richter and conductor Fritz Reiner.

Because it can be difficult to be inspired night after night, a sometimes-unrecognized hindrance to Artistry is when fine professional performers resort to *feigning* their involvement with the music, thus robbing their listeners of complete and honest fulfillment.[8] Fabricated engagement with the music is not only an issue for touring pianists, who must rise to the occasion completely alone onstage, but also perhaps for section orchestra players, should they come to feel that their inspired task is merely a routine job. It is less of a problem for chamber musicians, who have partners onstage while playing individual roles.

Performing which is possibly most damaging for the cause of music is that which is supremely professional, but soulless. Listeners are lured by the stunning skills of the performer(s), who can comfortably play at high speeds with the ultimate in technical smoothness and finesse. But inside, the performing has little musical depth, purpose, or potential to truly inspire. (Current examples include the recordings of some renowned Baroque ensembles.) Such perfect but hollow playing—emerging from performers others often look up to—is particularly dangerous for the future of music as a sublime language and art.[9]

---

8 Perhaps even the great Sergei Rachmaninoff succumbed during the countless times he felt obligated to perform his own famous *Prelude in C# Minor, Opus 3, No. 2*. Referring to the piece in a 1921 interview, he said: "I have become very tired of it. I feel like a little girl who is just learning to play and who knows only one piece...and I am often sorry I wrote it. I can never, never escape from a concert hall without playing it. It pursues me everywhere."

9 Performers should not aspire to be efficient score generators, but fully adopt their indispensable roles as thinking and feeling *creators*. Unfortunately, this crucial distinction is not always understood or appreciated by consumers (including classical music radio hosts), who often unquestioningly settle for the mundane and temporal in professional performances.

Toward the acceptance of freedom in score **interpretation**, it is helpful to recognize that there are really only two absolutes in written music: pitches (sounds) and rhythmic values. Other score directives (e.g. *tempo, dynamics*) are relative, needing to be determined by the decisions of each performer in meeting the perceived intentions of the music.

How best can we discuss these issues with our students and peers? To do so is made more difficult than is generally recognized, by the circumstance that there are language problems as well, as together we shall see.

CHAPTER TWO

Communication

Demaree

Words convey meaning, and thus matter greatly. Music conveys meaning, and thus matters greatly. But the two—words and music—never share cognates. Thus, they fail to translate each other into equivalent and precise synonyms. Varied shadings are needed to more sharply explain each, but these shadings can muddle and confuse even further any attempts at translation between these two distinct and expressive communication systems.

The late, great Robert Shaw once remarked that "It is no use getting philosophical" with the players in the Cleveland Orchestra. (Shaw was assistant to George Szell at the time, and was preparing to conduct Mozart and Stravinsky at Severance Hall.) "They just want to know," he said over his plate of pasta at his favorite Italian restaurant, "whether you want it faster or slower or louder or softer!" EN 2-1

Almost every musician who has struggled with congratulating a performer or composer, especially a fledgling, has thought

"What can I say that won't offend?" and has known the embarrassment of stammering merely that what has just been heard in concert was "…interesting.…" The underlying problem is that there is little enough precision in the conversations of musicians, even in professional settings, and the language by which musicians communicate with students and among their peers may be the most confusing of all the disciplines. Perhaps within no other field do its participants speak so knowledgeably and with such confident certainty, yet in more confused terms. There is a general atmosphere of relying on "what everyone knows" that is largely unjustified.

This characteristic inexactitude of vocabulary tends to isolate the Arts from the Sciences within Academe, and to make critical discourse relatively inexplicable to common folk. Scientists and other academics are, in general, committed to proof based on evidence—evidence that is evaluated with care and employed with rigorous accuracy. It was because Copernicus could not accept "what everyone knows" that civilization's sixteenth-century view of our solar system had to be revised. It was because Newton could not accept the simplistic seventeenth-century dictum that "apples naturally fall down" that our understanding of gravity emerged. (What is "natural," first of all?) It was because Einstein and others could not convince themselves that Newton's view—of an intertwining of Time and Space—was final, that the twentieth century had to reconsider both concepts.

It is far too easy simply to accept traditional, subjective language about Music without asking whether a further, newer precision is possible. Many teachers teach as they were taught, and they adopt the words and analogies that were useful when they themselves were students. So, another generation, and another, and then another, struggle to apply old forms of explanation that are relevant only if the student guesses correctly what the teacher is implying. The result too often can be regrettable. Thus, in the classroom or studio, to quote the classic line from the film *Cool Hand Luke,* "What we have here is a failure to communicate!" [EN 2-2]

The standard defense is that the Arts are different: "One simply cannot be precise about such 'ephemeral' matters, can one? Are these issues not matters of 'feeling,' and is there not an element of mystery around them?" Arts professionals would be frightened by any similar imprecision in the speech of their physicians or auto mechanics.

Why Verbal Communication about Music is Difficult

Speech requires *words*, and Music is uniquely *Music,* as we are stressing here. [EN 2-3] Centuries of aesthetic scholarship have as yet given us no efficient translation from the one to the other, and none is likely to emerge. [EN 2-4]

In music, a major triad does not translate to "happy," nor a minor one to "sad;" the two sonorities simply are what they are. And since there are no cognates between music and textual language, any attempt to explain in words what a passage of music "means" is risky and at best imprecise.

This difficulty of communicating is magnified by a distracting dichotomy between physical skills, on the one hand, and **Artistry**, on the other.[1] Since at least some **technique** must be

---

1   Again, each of the words defined as technical terms will appear in **bold type** when first used in each chapter, for the sake of the reader, who is thus reminded to refer afresh as needed to the Glossary.

established in any medium before either a younger or more mature musician can engage successfully in freedom of expression, early student tutelage must generally focus on drilling these physical skills (just as field officers in the military must teach and practice repeatedly with their troops the relationships between such elementary command words as "Right Face!" and "Halt" and the unified actions desired).

At any level of study, students and teachers first communicate together through the vocabularies of (1) technique (tonguings, bowing styles, embouchures, and fingerings, for example), (2) basic notated signs (*mf, p, allegro, marcato,* etc.), and (3) practice procedures. Students must generally focus on drilling basic skills (e.g. scales, arpeggios) before increasingly shifting their attention to matters of **style** and expression. Students and teachers must then hope to share a language of **expressivity**.

But in the absence of a shared language, the substitute in many studios historically has been imitation. [EN 2-5] When a student plays a passage in a tasteless way, the teacher's voice, or violin, or trumpet is quickly at the ready, and an **interpretation** the teacher prefers can be easily and perhaps wordlessly demonstrated. It is, of course, primarily for this pragmatic reason that piano studios customarily are equipped with a second instrument. Recordings also can be employed, often in a library or on the Internet, without the awareness—sometimes regrettably—of the teacher. Performances by visiting artists can have a strong impact. Each of these offers the student a chance to emulate a privately-accepted style without requiring verbal communication. But this is not always the best way. (Wider discussion of imitation will be found in Chapter 11, Stage and Studio: A Brief Word on Teaching.)

There is one circumstance in which full freedom of expression is not encouraged. Ensemble work—from chamber music to symphonies and opera—demands of its performers shared interpretational choices. Even concerto artists, let alone orchestra members and string quartet players, must collaborate, and often they have to do so without productive oral discussion of alternatives. (They do not generally seek to build shared vocabularies, either.)

Finally—since the days of Neapolitan opera, at least, as well as with the idolized solo "stars" of the nineteenth century—it has been financially advantageous for famous conductors and performers to encourage a public illusion that great musicians are somehow other-worldly. Instead of conversing frankly about their interpretive ideas, they have often deliberately created a mystique that they are personally "bringing Art down from Sinai under a divine dispensation." In this context, Artistry is retailed as if it were a "terra incognita" which cannot be discussed, only admired.

Useless and Confusing Words

Some of the handful of words which might be employed to express Artistic viewpoints have been used—and overused— so carelessly as to become ineffectual.

"**Musical**" and "**musicality**" are two such. Typically, these are employed by teachers and competition-judges to identify young people who appear to them to have "expressive-potential" (as opposed to mere technical agility). Score sheets for school contest judges often include, for example, a category labelled "musicianship." EN 2-6

Like "love" or "nice" or "beautiful", the English word "musical" has too many broad applications to be clearly used with a specific purpose; beyond its popular application to "Broadway light opera," it can be used to describe "melodious speech," or an **expressive** performance. The word has even been used to compliment listeners whose responses to a performance seem to show special affinity. It signifies, at best, the ability to hear, understand, and respond to music. It is distinct from "**talent**."

For our purposes herein, "talent" and "**talented**" also have little specific value. They refer variously to inborn qualities—especially suggesting potential—which cannot be taught. There are simply too many possible elements (including physical qualities) for these words to provide much information. The public uses the terms broadly, however, and so do many professional musicians. EN 2-7 The word "talent" is thus commonly used disingenuously.[2]

Perhaps it is "**phrasing**" that is confusingly employed most often. It is a word seldom used by listeners. Singers and wind players commonly mean no more by "phrasing" (or "phrase this passage") than to breathe at a logical point; other instrumentalists often mean "think like a singer." At best this word can imply an element of interpretation. The noun "phrase" is generally applied by music theorists to the "shortest structural unit ended by a cadence," and for them the word signifies nothing with respect to breathing. We suggest that a better term might be to "shape" these shortest structural units into a beautiful line.

---

2 Author Demaree recalls an entrepreneur's "talent" exam; the pitchman acknowledged that the purpose of the exam was to sell his new electronic organs to the parents of children who demonstrated "talent"—which they could do by simply facing the keys when asked to sit on the bench. None of these "auditionees" ever failed this test, of course, and many of the families did buy electronic organs.

Scripted Artistry?

If there were only a single precise expression that could be produced aptly for each moment of an original work, it would seem possible for the composer to notate every wish on the handwritten manuscript (if composers really wanted that sort of **rigidity**). But of course, it is not possible to notate everything so thoroughly, nor is notation complete music. It is, furthermore, one of the very strengths of Music that varied interpretations are of great value, bringing fresh and often deepened meaning to a given work.

Composers in the Baroque and Classical eras did not even try. They marked their manuscripts very economically, if at all, and left performance choices to those who would undertake their scores.

Many composers in the nineteenth and twentieth centuries appeared to be frustrated with the limitations of standard notation, marking their scores more rigidly and sometimes virtually clothing performers in interpretive straitjackets. From the sparse or absent dynamic indications of the Renaissance, Baroque, and Classical eras, the Romantics, Impressionists, and their successors moved on to more and more specific symbols— *ffff, pppp,* extravagant tempo markings, ties from cadential notes to short "cut-off notes" (to control exact releases), and similarly-invented signals of all sorts. [EN 2-8] An example of extensive score markings from the standard piano literature is the Sonata Opus 1 (1909) by Alban Berg, a fine work which contains extremely precise, nonstop instructions for numerous performance matters such as timing and dynamics.

By the mid-twentieth century the Electronic School had

gained the technological prowess to do away with live performance entirely, and some declared that the composer would now be able to control every parameter absolutely.

All these efforts to control **interpretation** represented, to a certain extent, a suspicion of the expressive freedom that traditional notation had left to performers. In some quarters the performer was no longer viewed as a partner to the composer, but rather as a servant expected to attempt to reproduce the master's original ideas precisely. (We had come very far from the worlds of C. P. E. Bach and Leopold Mozart.)

But audiences preferred the excitement and revivification of live performance, and the "revolt of the composers" was stymied. If the composers could not make all performances of a work—historical or contemporary—reflect one precise and limited set of expressive choices, then live performers would again have to be encouraged to sensitively and intelligently interpret the music from the composers' notated scores. (Jazz musicians had always endorsed these sorts of freedoms, and from their word "square" we still derive their image of cold, rigid, and insensitive performance.) Yet at the same moment, the world (or era) in which a particular historic composer lived should—must—be reestablished and made recognizable in performance.

One of the present authors' principal concerns is to clarify in what ways rigid, mechanical, or colorless performance can be helped to be imaginative and expressive (that is, given "personality"), without encouraging excess. This process which we call "interpreting" inevitably involves adding to the music something not specifically present in the notation. Ideally, it requires (1) broad knowledge of the composer's catalog and of the works of his contemporaries, (2) judgment about **taste** and style as current among other (and historic) performers of this literature, (3) sufficiently deft physical skills to achieve one's insights, (4) imagination and **pliability**, both limited by the factors just listed, and (5) a lack of inhibitions that would block **interpretive** freedom. All of this fosters **expressivity**.

The difficulties Robert Shaw experienced in conveying his wishes to the Cleveland Orchestra is symptomatic—and still endemic. Musicians remain in much the same circumstance as the European explorers who first encountered unknown languages while attempting to find the sources of the Nile. We can do better at this than we have been doing.

PART II

Interpretive Studies

There are few absolute rules about playing Shakespeare, but many possibilities . . . We don't believe there's only one way of doing Shakespeare—that way madness lies.

- John Barton [EN II-1]

Let us now make it our purpose to look at and listen to some specific passages of widely different works by a panoply of great composers, seeking to encourage **Artistry** through freedom and individual exploration. How can we generalize about this endeavor?

Near the end of his distinguished concert career, American pianist John Browning opined in an interview that if he could do it all over again, he would dedicate himself to simply following what is written on the music score. [EN II-2]

There are other such clichés. Noted German baritone Matthias Goerne said in a recent newspaper interview: "The key to finding the right way for a piece is…finding the right way in the score, because 95% is already there from the composer. We have just this *little* part, to make the sound and do it as right as possible." [EN II-3]

Consider an alternative approach. Once upon a time there was a towering teacher, the late Prof. Julius Herford: scholar, conductor, pianist, coach of Robert Shaw, Lukas Foss, Roger Wagner, and later two or three generations of other young conductors. (Herford's influence thus today is legend, and beyond borders.) It was he who first brought to the attention of the present authors the concept he called "the **Spiral Study**." EN II-4

How does an aspiring **Artist** first approach a work that is relatively unknown to her/him? Herford's approach was invariably (1) begin with the text (if any) and have the notated original score of that work at hand, (2) familiarize oneself with other similar and dissimilar works by the same composer (from the same period, and then earlier and later), (3) study the culture and history of the locale and period, (4) study representative works by contemporary and earlier composers, (5) and thus in ever-diverging "spirals" gradually gain a sprawling contextual foundation for the work of one's original focus. These are formidable, even exhaustive tasks, which can help performers understand the music more thoroughly and develop divergent approaches to a given work over the years.

Herein the present authors could compare, and contrast works in any genre (that is to say, music written for any instrument or ensemble), but have arbitrarily chosen solo piano works. The issues on which we will focus are the same, after all, for a passage from a Beethoven piano sonata, a Bach solo cello suite, or a movement from a Brahms symphony. Our examples will range widely across the established piano literature from Bach to Bartók. Author Demaree will give each composer and work brief historical, biographical, and theoretical contexts, framing multiple passages from the chosen works which will be performed and discussed with voice-over commentary by pianist/author Hamilton.* Hamilton's commentary will also be printed in the text at the conclusion of each composer chapter.

It is not our intent in Part II to consider the composers chronologically, but rather to focus on them as unique individuals, each displaying his own personality. Part III will then attempt to coalesce, discuss and expand these insights, offering a general theory of interpretation.

* Recorded performances and commentary
may be found online at:
www.roberthamiltonpianist.com
Artistry

CHAPTER THREE

An Emigrant from Warsaw

Frédéric Chopin: *F Minor Ballade, op. 52*

Demaree

The year 1810, when both Fryderyk Franciszek Chopin and Robert Schumann were born, was perhaps the peak of power for Napoleonic France. The self-proclaimed Emperor had re-drawn much of the map of Europe; his fleet battled with the Royal Navy at sites around the globe, and his disastrous Russian invasion was still two years in the future. During the next decade he would capture Moscow, lose crucial battles at Leipzig and Waterloo, and experience imprisonment himself at both nearby Elba and distant St. Helena.

Over that decade *la belle France* would begin its long nineteenth- and twentieth-century slide from having become (with the Emperor's annexation of the Netherlands) a virtual synonym for "Western Europe," suffering recurring military defeats that led to German, English, Nazi, American, and other foreign troops parading under the *Arc de Triomphe*. Its overseas possessions would remain relatively unaffected until the revolution-based losses of Algeria and Vietnam. Two centuries of spiritual malaise and political posturing finally left the culture a largely agrarian society, with little to offer in twenty-first century international affairs save pretense.

In 1810-1830, Chopin's homeland, Poland, became a *former*

Frédéric Chopin, from a photograph by Louis-Auguste Bisson, circa 1849

Poland Zelazowa Wola, Chopin birthplace

country, not an independent nation. Three surrounding powers—Imperial Russia, the Habsburg Empire, and the Prussian state of Frederick the Great—had hungrily absorbed the whole of Poland by the end of the previous century, so that it disappeared from maps of Europe until the end of World War I, over a century later. The

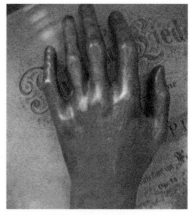

Chopin's hand, postmortem cast, Polish Museum, Rapperswil, Switzerland

Grave of Chopin in Paris, France

three conquering powers would not themselves be punished decisively for this rapacious statecraft until the destruction of the Soviet Empire in the 1980s, almost two centuries later.

Such a long purgatory made of Chopin's homeland an icon *romantique,* and heightened the poignancy of his "Polish works," which he crafted with an apparent eye to mourning his people's pain. (As an American pianist says, Chopin's ethnic works "all tell a tale.") EN 3-1 The very geophysical identity of "Poland" was disadvantageous: its location between these great powers led politicians to regard the Polish plains as easy routes to conquest. This historic circumstance would remind one of the purported reply by the King of the Belgians in 1914 to the German Army's request for free passage to the northwestern French border. His inspired response "Belgium is a nation, not a road!" was to be reflected when Polish cavalry—in 1939 still on horseback—charged Nazi tanks and artillery twenty-five years later. Such ineffectual gallantry would reappear through the twentieth century in the Nazi/Soviet shift of Poland to the west, the Berlin Airlift, the massive forced population migrations, and the building of the temporary Berlin Wall. In the end, a relocated Poland would live again.

• • •

Paris during Napoleon I's rule and thereafter had become visibly the political capital of Europe, and manifestly the rival of Vienna as its artistic center. The beauties from the past—*La Sainte Chappelle, Notre Dame, Montparnasse,* the boulevards, the parks, the *Seine,* and all—were woven together with the palaces of the nobility and the mansions of the wealthy (each of which could be expected to include a "music room" or a modest concert hall). It must have occurred to young Chopin and his elite Warsaw friends that a handsome young pianist could do very well in the great city. Presenting himself as "Frédéric" Chopin, he brought his already-heralded talent from his native Poland (prideful and rustic) to Paris (grand and sophisticated), the splendid capital of Louis-Philippe I, who had been ruler of France for about a year at that point. The bright young Pole now signed his name "Frédéric François," (a bit of marketing skill already evident there!) and began to exhibit the manner and customs of his new homeland. He was just twenty-one.

Nevertheless, any assessment of the work of Frédéric Chopin commences with an almost-obligatory deference to his Polish heritage, and places emphasis on his devotion to the land of his birth. Thus it may surprise some readers to learn that Chopin (generally thought today to have been born in 1810 in a village near Warsaw) left his native land at an early age, and chose to dwell in Paris and Mediterranean lands for the remaining half of his life. He deliberately fostered a public image as a Polish patriot by composing and emphasizing "Polish works," in Paris and elsewhere (as he had in Warsaw) throughout his career. Among his very first published works was a batch of *Mazurkas*; the *Polonaise-fantaisie in A-flat, op. 61* [EN 3-2] was one of his last. (Note these ethnic, perhaps even jingoistic, titles.)

Beginning in 1831-32, his output was largely cosmopolitan, with *concerti, scherzi,* songs, and chamber music alternating with nationalistic works. Among these were *Polonaises, etc.,* leading up to the aforementioned *Polonaise-fantaisie in A-flat.* Note that, alone among major composers, Chopin never published a work which did not incorporate the piano.

Of the "cosmopolitan" works, the *F Minor Ballade, op. 52,* is the capstone (1842) of four such titles. These *Ballades* do not bear ethnic soubriquets from his native land, and all four date from his early Parisian years: the *G Minor, op. 23,* was the first, likely written after 1832, and the other three followed within a decade. The predominating structural design of the period, the so-called *sonata allegro* form, was widely regarded as a succession of contrasting melodies, more-or-less incidentally scored in related keys; it was taught as such, especially at the *Paris Conservatoire.* Yet in fact, as designed in the eighteenth century this was not so; the sonata form was *not* constructed around a succession of melodies. It was, instead, a scheme of contrasting keys. "One searches in vain through… writings of the time for the familiar thematic outline found in today's textbooks." [EN 3-3]

Enough time had passed since the legendary figures of Classical Vienna departed the scene that those seeking fresh forms and ideas were now edging away from the designs even of Beethoven. Especially they sought new key relationships, new blueprints, and even new audiences. Samson assures us that "sonata form is the essential reference point for all four ballades," but then he hastens to qualify that statement. "Rondo and variation elements certainly were present." We would suggest for the latter era the overall term *Sonata-fantaisie*, prompted particularly by the rather strict presentation and refining of the pre-eminent themes, emblazoned with more-and-more demanding displays of **technique** as the pianist nears the end of the work. (The first and fourth Ballades are especially clear examples of this sort of volcanic coda.)

Of course, the Chopin catalogue is not all sonatas, ballades, sets of variations, or other longer works. In his roster, dance forms (*mazurkas*, waltzes, *polonaises*, etc.) predominate, along with nocturnes and etudes. These shorter works have made him a favorite of recitalists and their audiences for almost two centuries now. Delight can come in small packages.

How rigidly did Chopin himself view the performance of his own scores? Not very, according to numerous reports by those who heard him play. Noted pianist Byron Janis wrote an article [EN 3-4] in which he recounted the experience of Julius Seligmann, then president of the Glasgow Society of Musicians, who attended a recital where the composer played his own *Mazurka in B-flat, op. 7, no. 1* as an encore. "It met with such great success that Chopin decided to play it again, this time with such a radically different **interpretation**—*tempi,* colors and phrasing all changed—that it sounded like an entirely different piece. The audience was amazed when it finally realized he was playing the very same *mazurka....*"

The *F Minor Ballade, op. 52,* is the last (1842) of the four ballades he composed, and is generally regarded as one of his finest creations.

For recorded performance & commentary, please visit:
www.roberthamiltonpianist.com
Artistry: 1. *F Minor Ballade, op. 52*

Quatrième Ballade.

à Mme la Baronne C. de ROTHSCHILD.

F. CHOPIN. Op. 52.

Recorded Voice-over remarks (printed version)

Hamilton

This performance recording aims to demonstrate some of the important aspects of artistic interpretation which have been presented in the text. While listening, please keep these factors in mind:

- **First,** Artistry uses the written score as an unfinished image and point of departure;
- **Second,** a dozen Artists, each with the primary and over-riding goal of expressing the composer's intentions, will come up with as many worthy, but different solutions;
- **Third,** Artistry is as much about expressing the *thoughts* behind the sounds as the sounds themselves. This is critical if one is to respect music as a language which bears meaningful messages; and
- **Fourth,** while expressing each individual moment, performers must keep the greater overall message of the work in mind, or risk creating a number of beautiful parts that fail to add up to an intelligent structural whole.

[*Note that the ellipses (series of dots) in the material which follows indicate a performed musical example in the recording.*]

We begin with Chopin, one of the most **intuitive** of composers, requiring in turn a free and intuitive approach. Among Chopin's most compelling and beautiful creations is the fourth *Ballade*. Yet I wonder how many would conclude this when presented with the rhythm of its opening theme.......... Well then, there surely must be variety in the melody pitches of the theme. Let's put rhythm and melodic line together.......... Still pretty monotonous. Harmony is the true color of music, so let's now add that as well. Here is what a pianist might come up with if the overriding intent was to simply follow what is in the written score......... If you followed along with the score, you will have noted that the dynamics, articulation and time markings were faithfully executed. And the result is, indeed, beautiful. But would we call this Artistry? Let's compare what you just heard with this.......... You will note that I used more **interpretive** freedom this time, for example, with the rhythm. One might complain that we shouldn't play around with Chopin's written rhythms, to which I might ask "Why should we think Chopin would want us to perform his music in a restrictive manner very different from his own approach?" In the text we have quoted some who heard Chopin play, referencing the great liberties he took. And we also read the advice of Chopin himself, to avoid playing something the same way twice. We should celebrate the fact that Chopin, and other composers, did not attempt to write in every specific nuance for us to follow! Keep in mind that the variety of potential interpretations is one of the hallmark strengths of the performed arts. Let's hear three sample interpretations of the C major theme as different Artists might express it. We will begin with the version you just heard, which makes the most of dynamic expressive possibilities.......... Perhaps Artist Two wants not to make a statement with this theme, so much as to provide a breezy introduction, and selects a quicker speed for the *Andante con moto*.......... And yet a third Artist takes a much slower, rhythmically freer and intimate approach.......... As always with the markings from the composer, we have only a general idea of what speed he meant by *Andante con moto*. These second and third samples are probably nearing the outer limits of fast and slow, and need careful handling. As we move along, you will also notice that much more than what we discuss is being changed from version to version. This includes the message behind the sounds, as well as the sounds themselves.

Continuing with the *Ballade*, here is the first part of the f minor theme played strictly as it appears on paper.......... Respectful, good sound and character. Now consider what a bit of tweaking might provide.......... Or for those who prefer more motion.......... Although these are just brief glimpses, you can probably hear how the performance flexibility of either latter version would wear better than the first over the entire length of the piece. Here is the way this first phrase might sound in the two latter versions with accompaniment added, the quicker one first this time.......... Now taking just the cadence, or third part of the phrase, let's look at how small changes of stress, or a pause, can alter the shape of things.......... Next I will play the entire f minor theme in four different manners, as you might hear from four different Artists. Note that while the visions differ, each being very expressive, all of them will seem to belong to a larger vision and will avoid circling too much around select moments. In part, this will be because of my determination not to be pulled into a new central tempo. The differences you hear will include tempo, the varying degree of *rubato*, dynamic levels and nuance, plus the relayed messages behind the sounds..........To conclude with a broader perspective, I will play from the *Ballade's* beginning until the end of the first two f minor theme groups. There will be many wide freedoms taken, from *tempi* to *rubati* and stress points. Listen especially for these several factors:

- flexibility of time and nuance, rather than a straight reading of the score;
- a sense that there is a vision behind the notes; and
- a willingness to apply broad contrasts, but not permitting even the most expressive of them to distract from the larger destination and message.......

Moral

Are some still enmeshed in the "ideal interpretation" theory? We must use all of our intuitive gifts! Chopin was too great a musician to limit his own creative judgment with mere notation. Let us avoid **rigidity**, employing full expressive insight and intellect.

CHAPTER FOUR
The Thunderer from Bonn

Ludwig van Beethoven: *Sonate für das Pianoforte, op. 109*

Demaree

Almost exactly four decades earlier another young pianist, having impressed the gentry of his hometown (like Warsaw, a somewhat limited artistic environment) left the Rhenish realm of his birth for a distant city, another great capital. Just as the youthful Chopin had moved to Paris from Eastern Europe at age twenty-one, so the pianist from Bonn—young Ludwig van Beethoven, not yet twenty-two himself—journeyed eastward to Imperial Vienna, ostensibly to study with Joseph Haydn. Like Chopin, he would remain in his new environment for most of the rest of his life.

There were other parallels between the two: Chopin had come from a proud culture, but compared to Paris a somewhat provincial one, and Beethoven from an unpretentious city on the Rhine. Both composed at an early age, and both became legendary for their exciting skills at improvisation. Both found early success and life-long patronage. Both came to their capital cities rather less than sophisticated, but both coolly and calculatedly found voices who would speak for them among the social elite, and even the nobility. In the end, however, it was Chopin's emerging sophistication and Beethoven's explosive power that made both of them tower in the nineteenth century's salons and concert halls.

Beethoven from a painting by Joseph Karl Stieler, 1820

The first real difficulty for the rough-hewn Beethoven was that his great mentor had not yet passed from the scene; Haydn was in his early seventies when "young" (thirty-five-ish) Beethoven's great years began, and by then the old man's career had peaked with the "London Symphonies" plus his two great oratorios. At this point Beethoven had reached Haydn's level (with the "*Pathétique*" Sonata, op. 13, the "*Waldstein*", and the "*Appassionata*", for example),

Portrait of Ludwig van Beethoven by Johann Peter Lyse

and the younger man was ready to seek expression for even more grandiose and profound concepts: the *Missa solemnis*, the late quartets, the "Ninth," the late keyboard works, etc.

In 1820, as if with a relieved sigh, Ludwig van Beethoven turned from the piano sonata he had most recently composed (the massive *"Hammerklavier" Sonata No. 29, in B-flat, op. 106*) to a concise work dedicated to his "little friend" Fraülein Maximilian Brentano. This would prove to be, by contrast, the compact *Sonata No. 30, in E, op. 109*, the first of his great trilogy. Beethoven had perhaps surprised himself by devoting a full year (1817-18) to the *"Hammerklavier."* There are subtle indications that he wanted now to free himself: for example, the compression to which he turned in op. 109 by

Life mask of Ludwig van Beethoven, c. 1812, The Welcome Collection, London

House where Beethoven was born in Bonn, Germany

offering just three movements (the *"Hammerklavier"* has four), the first and second of which are quite short. Note also that tonally the B-flat of *No. 29* vs. *No. 30*'s E major are as far apart as possible—a full tritone. It is as if he is saying "Let me leave that long sonata behind, and do something quite different!"[1]

Here is another demand on one's **intuition**: Music unfolds across time; hence the choice of *tempi* is among the most critical interpretive decisions for any work. For most movements composed before 1800 a single tempo throughout was probably intended (in keeping with the by-then-obsolete Baroque "Doctrine of the Affections.") Increasingly after that date, contrasting *tempi* may be stipulated within a single movement, of course, and relationships between them must be determined; *rubato* treatments may be implied, as well.[2]

---

1 The multiplicity of names for the principal keyboard instruments during the Classical era can be confusing: for example, "*Hammerklavier*" (German for "Pianoforte"). In this volume we coalesce "*fortepiano*" (Italian for "loudsoft") and "*pianoforte*" ("softloud") into the simple, modern English title/nickname "piano." "*Gravicembalo*" ("harpsichord with soft and loud") was actually the original name given to Bartolomeo Cristofori's 1700 keyboard invention by the poet/journalist Scipione Maffei. Although "pianoforte" and "fortepiano" were titles used interchangeably during the eighteenth and much of the nineteenth centuries, beginning in the mid-nineteenth century with the invention of the cast-iron plate (and other developments that changed the instrument dramatically), the title "fortepiano" was increasingly reserved for the early, more delicate instruments—as is true today. [EN 4-1]

2 It is well known that Beethoven had an early metronome, and today it is generally considered that either his own device or his use of it was inaccurate. (It was just in these years—in 1816, in Paris—that Maelzel began manufacturing his instruments.)[EN 4-2] Accurate or not, the metronome readings of Beethoven's era are generally not to be trusted. Decisions in this realm of *tempi* are artistic matters, and have great influence on both structure and line. Under the whole realm of "articulation," *rubato* effects, *tenuti*, *fermati*, and similar momentary gestures are related, since they provide opportunities for emphases, and blur any **rigidity** of tempo. A mere change of performance halls can make substantial tempo differences necessary, as can other factors. [EN 4-3]

Detailed Structure of the Opening Movement

In this study it is not (and should not be) our purpose to do a theoretical analysis in detail of every movement of each of our exemplary works. Our treatment of the Chopin *Fourth Ballade* was typical of our needs in this study, yet what follows here is an example of what we believe should be part of the preparation of every performer who approaches a new work.

The inventory of movement designs which had been sufficient for the eighteenth-century Viennese had seemed increasingly stifling to Beethoven as he matured. Joseph Haydn, in fact, already had commingled these designs freely in his later works, interweaving the shapes and spans of developmental forms, *rondo*, fugal, and variational designs in movement after movement. For some time the aging rebel from Bonn had been heading in the then-radical direction described immediately below.

The opening movement of the *Sonata No. 30 in E major* is a traditional sonata-allegro form, made revolutionary by the abrupt shift of its opening *Vivace, ma non troppo, Sempre legato* tempo (for the A material, marked *dolce*) to a momentarily bewildering *Adagio espressivo* for the B material, after just eight-and-a-half measures! Recalling the long spans of *op. 106*, one's initial reaction to this compact design is likely to be that "it begins in the character of a fantasia of some sort." The severe change of tempo at bar nine comes so soon that a listener is hardly ready to establish and compare images of structural units, yet the exposition is at that moment already half complete! Final affirmation that this is a classic sonata-allegro movement comes with the return of the B material in the tonic key at measure fifty-eight. In, say, the initial movement of the *Waldstein*, op. 53, a decade-and-a-half earlier, Beethoven took thirty-four measures to simply reach the B material. Here in measure fourteen he is already making something of a traditional closing to end the exposition.

At bar sixteen the A material begins again, in the dominant. The materials are inverted in this development, and then elaborated at bar twenty-two; there with *sempre legato* and *cresc.* stipulations he commences a masterful, mostly conjunct ascent to the original dominant at the highest reaches of his keyboard. After six-and-a-half measures of what is an inverted pedalpoint on that B-natural, he returns the A material to the original key as a traditional recapitulation (but a climactic two octaves higher!). Now at fifty-eight comes that reprise of the B material (still beginning *Adagio espressivo*), down a fifth from its original statement and thus characteristically set in the tonic key, with the original closing from sixty-three to sixty-five.

Halfway through measure sixty-six comes a coda at *tempo primo*, but marked this time *legato*, rather than the *dolce* of the opening and bar fifteen. Beethoven veers toward the dominant for this reprise, and turns the passage into a second development. In bar seventy-six he slows the pace for eleven measures of quarter-note chords, and then closes the movement with a variant of A for twelve bars to the final chord (marked *fermata*).

The overall shape of the movement (which has no introduction, of course) is a fifteen-bar exposition (completed by a rather fantasia-like B section), some thirty-four measures of development, eighteen of recapitulation, and thirty-four bars of coda—a design remarkable in the Viennese Classical style post-Haydn [EN 4-4] for only two features: its extreme brevity, and the division of the exposition into two starkly-different tempi.

(Compare this with the duration of the first movement of the *Sonata Pathétique, Op. 13, in C Minor*. There too the design is original, and the apparent introduction turns out to be focal material in the structure of the first movement.)

The remainder of *op. 109* is just as distinctive. The second movement, a *prestissimo*, emerges out of the pedaled *fermata* of the previous movement, and proves to be another sonata-allegro structure. Beethoven was no slave to textbook forms, and he sought to use the principles within such designs in imaginative ways—increasingly in his final string quartets, for example—as we have just observed in the opening movement. This *finale* is one of the grandest achievements of perhaps the greatest master of the variations structure.

Let us return to the keyboard and the spoken word.

For recorded performance & commentary, please visit:
www.roberthamiltonpianist.com
Artistry: 2. Beethoven *Sonata, Op. 109*

SONATE
für das Pianoforte
von

L. van BEETHOVEN.

Fräulein Maximiliana Brentano gewidmet.
Op. 109.

Vivace. mà non troppo. Sempre legato.

Sonate No. 30.

Adagio espressivo.

Original-Verleger: A. M. Schlesinger in Berlin.   B. 153.   Stich und Druck von Breitkopf & Härtel in Leipzig.

B. 153.

Recorded Voice-over remarks (printed version)

Hamilton

While it might be said that the **intuitive** probings of Chopin are sounds in search of shape or formal structure, Beethoven comes from the other side: beginning with a structure like sonata-allegro form and filling it with selected sounds. Beethoven composed a large number of first movements in sonata form, and in his later years he experimented. One such experiment is the first movement of his *opus 109 sonata in E major*. Here he uses an extremely condensed/compact sonata form, giving us a perfect example for use within the constraints of time.

A typical Beethoven first movement, whether piano sonata, symphony or piece of chamber music, will consist of some fifty bars for the first theme group (one hundred bars when the repeat is taken). In *op. 109*, this length is reduced to a meager eight-and-a-half bars, and there is no repeat! Thus, the performer has to prepare carefully for a very abrupt surprise, or interruption. We are aided by the simple/naïve nature of the first theme, which skips along as if it might go on forever, before a dark cloud cancels out the sunshine........ Once again, as with the Chopin, there are many choices an **Artist** can make to express this drama. Since this first theme goes by so fast, thought needs to go into determining what the performer believes Beethoven wishes to say. There are many ways to begin. Here are five potential openings among numerous choices. The first is positive, but naïve....... this one is uncertain/tentative....... the third has a bit of a swagger....... and yet another skips lightly and is more child-like....... and a fifth might be taken by those wishing to emphasize a more formal sonata opening.......

For the second half of this brief theme, things get even more interesting. Coming just before the sharp intrusion, should we perhaps convey naïve confidence....... or some boldness....... Then what of the nature of the interrupting diminished chord which initiates the second theme group in bar nine? Should it be, perhaps, deeply thoughtful....... or ruthless....... or ominous....... For the full second theme, we might choose a refined/thoughtful rendition....... or a more emotional one showing sympathy and a touch of anger....... Moving along a bit less slowly would bring another meaning.......

Turning to the development, should we pay more attention to getting back to the original tempo (*i.e.,* moving along again)......or should we probe more with respect to the *dolce* marking....... Earlier we mentioned that op. 109's shorter proportions offer a good opportunity to consider what I would call the important second and third rungs of **Artistry:** creating a balanced architecture, and expressing the message behind the notes. Here is one possible **interpretation** of the entire first movement, striving to observe Beethoven's carefully notated score in a full realization which brings thousands of subtleties which no score could (or should) try to present. Beethoven's road map is very clear and must be observed. But the journey itself is ours to make, needing to be embraced fully and lived by the performer in search of the intended message.......

"As personal afflictions—deafness and the inability to enter into happy personal relationships—loomed larger, he [Beethoven] began to compose in an increasingly personal musical style, and at the end of his life he wrote his most sublime and profound works. From his success at combining tradition, and exploration, and personal expression, he came to be regarded as the dominant musical figure of the nineteenth century...." [EN 4-5] The Fates gathered around him, and it became legendary that on his deathbed he shook his fist at the heavens. (Tongue-in-cheek, we suggest that perhaps he was demanding that God give him "more octaves on my Broadwood." That would have been characteristic of him.) Mozart and Haydn had to work with what was available to them. Beethoven was never ready to compromise.

Intuition and Improvisation

Beethoven built his early reputation in Wien by public improvisation, much as would Chopin in Paris. In so doing, both were focusing primarily on intuition, trusting their judgment about this ultimate reliance on imagination, as they conceived the whole form and the details of a new work. And like Chopin, Beethoven was too great a musician to fence in his own creativity with mere notation.

CHAPTER FIVE

A Mutual Admiration Society in Austria

Joseph Haydn: *Sonata in C, Hob. XVI/48*
Wolfgang Mozart: *Sonata in B-Flat, KV 333*

Demaree

From the time of the trudging of the legions along the valley of the Danube, long past the death of the great Emperor Marcus Aurelius at what by that time (c. 180 AD) was a Roman frontier post called Vindabona, through the centuries of political and economic domination of the Balkans by the great Habsburg capital now known as Vienna (Wien), the geographic importance of that city as a commercial junction made it a center for wealth, power, art, and music. Whatever and whoever travelled the great river east and west, or the pathways and later railroads south and north made use of the confluences of those media for business and pleasure. For most of three millennia, those seeking personal and/or economic advancement might very reasonably look for them there. For most of three millennia, and still today, those seeking to prosper north of Italy, including polished and exciting musicians and visual artists, could hope to find markets for their works in Vienna and its surroundings. The road from Venice, particularly, carried to Vienna the musical traditions that had marked forever the *Duomo San Marco* and its environs. EN 5-1

Portrait of Joseph Haydn, 1785 by Christian Ludwig Seehas

By the first half of the eighteenth century, almost all the ranking musicians in Europe and the British Isles could be encountered and heard passing through Vienna from time to time, competing in the rivalries that were part of its theatres and

House where Joseph Haydn was born, Karl Bobies

salons. (So even such a giant figure as Vivaldi would
come north from the
Adriatic to seek Habsburg
patronage and die.) ^{EN 5-2}

• • •

Occasionally in music
history greatness has come
in pairs: Bach and Handel,
Brahms and Wagner, and
perhaps the most surpris-
ing twosome, Haydn and

The Boy Mozart, anonymous painting
commissioned by Leopold Mozart (1763)

Mozart—surprising because these rivals were friends. Even

Mozart Family Portrait from a painting by Johann Nepomuk della Croce, c. 1780

beyond that, each seems to have believed the other was the greater master.

Mozart's father, Leopold, was born in 1719, and so he was virtually one of Haydn's own generation. On the other hand, Wolfgang Mozart himself was barely three years old when Prince Paul Anton Esterhazy, virtual viceroy of Hungary under the Habsburg regime, first appointed Haydn as *Kapellmeister* at his own court. Then Mozart's early death in 1791 preceded Haydn's own passing by eighteen years, coming when Beethoven was just twenty-one.

The early training of the two contrasted starkly: one of them, "Wolferl" Mozart, was given every elitist advantage. His childhood centered on the influential musicians in Salzburg, Paris, Vienna, London, and a "Grand Tour" of the famous of Italy. This youth played for the Empress Maria Theresa twice before he was seven, and his life began then to be legendary. Everyone who had *entrée* to meet and hear the lad play at the keyboard came away with an idolatrous story of the remarkable musical abilities he displayed. Some of their tales were even true! (He was said to have copied down from memory after just one hearing—or was it two?—the Papal Choir's private motet.) [EN 5-3] Yet his real abilities were, at his age, undeniably remarkable, and his proud father missed no opportunities to trumpet them.

Leopold Mozart was putatively the finest violinist in the world at the time, and author of the most important violin instruction book [EN 5-4] of the era. The child Wolfgang was surrounded by important musicians and teachers: Beyond his immediate family, he was part of a thriving musical community in Salzburg, where he, by the way, encountered and copied a mass by Michael Haydn. Among his first works in London are found (not surprisingly) some in the handwriting of his father. ^{EN 5-5} Just so, the influence of no less than Johann Christophe Bach himself (with whom Leopold and Wolfgang stayed for months in London in the mid-1760s) is manifest in Wolfgang's first symphonic writing. He was recognized as a child prodigy, ^{EN 5-6} of course, and would benefit from a growing "cloud of witnesses."

His own abilities were buttressed—at the least—by such instruction from many famous acquaintances. He seems to have been a diligent student: on another trip to Italy with his father, he received counterpoint lessons from the legendary Padre Martini in Bologna, and thus he approached fugal technique systematically. Late in his life, he would take advantage of a visit to Germany to continue that interest by learning from the scores of the master himself, Sebastian Bach, just as he had studied with that genius's youngest son.

• • •

For "Sepperl" (Joseph) Haydn the early years were also impressive, but very different from "Wolferl's" experiences. Born in a dirt-floored farmhouse (as Beethoven would note a generation later) in a humble village in 1732, Haydn would be "discovered" as a boy soprano at age five in a larger village, would move to the great St. Stephan's Cathedral in Vienna at about age eight, and would sing for a decade in the *Stephansdom* choir under the great *Kapellmeister* Karl Georg (von) Reutter the Younger (who was too busy with Viennese music and politics to give the boy the regular counterpoint and other lessons we are told he had promised him). "Sepperl's" post in Maria Theresa's court was a sophisticated and cosmopolitan one. ^{EN 5-7}

Little matter that Reutter was too busy to really spend much time teaching him! Young Haydn was what every master seeks: the boy seems to have been innately self-disciplined, on the way to self-taught. When the other choirboys went out to play, the aged Franz Joseph would recall that as a boy he would grasp a small *klavier* and carry it to a room where he could practice. When his soprano voice finally broke in late 1749 or early 1750, Reutter dismissed him from *Stephansdom*. Haydn spent the next decade free-lancing on the streets and in the churches of Vienna, amid a smorgasbord of musical activities: playing organs and leading choirs, playing evening serenades, accompanying, and even serving as a valet, blacking boots for his master.[1]

From age fifteen or so, still at *Stephansdom*, to the end of his decade on the streets (1760 or so) and on through his early years in the Esterhazy household, Haydn led the way in the formulation of what would come to be known famously as the Viennese Classical Style. This assemblage of principles and musical procedures would influence everyone from Mozart and Beethoven through Schubert, Brahms, and Berg to the present day. "Haydn's primary concern was to conceive architectural proportions for a design, and then to manipulate...through the passage of Time

---

1 With an eye to the future, the diligent youth read every important technical book he could buy or borrow: He devoured Fux's monumental *Gradus ad Parnassum* (1725), working its problems and annotating his copy for his students and friends. Among other famous studies he absorbed Carl Philip Emanuel Bach's *Versuch über die wahre Art das Clavier zu spielen,* and his *Prussian Sonatas* (1743), David Kellner's *Treulicher Unterricht in General-Bass* (1732), Leopold Mozart's renowned *Versuch einer gründlichen Violinschule* (1756), and Johann Mattheson's *Der volkommene Kapellmeister* (1739). All this careful preparation recalls the phrase attributed to young Abe Lincoln, reading before his cabin fireplace: "I will study and be ready, and some day my chance will come." [EN 5-8]

his listeners' expectations regarding those proportions. Haydn's structures are architectures of Time, with intermittent temporal landmarks toward which he directs his audiences." EN 5-9

Two chronologies were overlapping in the first third of Haydn's life: (1) as a soloist in Reutter's *Stephansdom* choir he was singing (expertly) and hearing every day the style of the High Renaissance, actually refining that style through the look-ing-glass of the *Gradus ad Parnassum* viewpoint of that era, as construed by Reutter's most prominent predecessor, Johann Fux (who did not intend to be a revolutionary, but to hand down the perfected techniques of Palestrina, Victoria, and the High Renaissance); and (2) especially after his dismissal from the cathedral, Haydn was hearing (performed by his young contemporaries) the new styles, known now for the last two centuries as the Neo-Classic transitional experiments, which even Reutter promulgated in some of his own works. Haydn, by 1760, clearly was searching for this new order, which would come to be known as the Viennese Classical style. EN 5-8

There is much uncertainty on one important point. We do not know exactly when Mozart and Haydn first met face to face. It must have been sometime in the 1780s, since the younger man's dedicatory letter to the older master covering the six "Haydn Quartets," dates from 1785, and the Michael Kelly "reminiscences" of the Haydn-Dittersdorf-Mozart-Vanhal "qu-artet evenings" refer to c.1784. EN 5-9 One speculation of ours of-fers an intriguing possibility: "Sepperl's" brother—the compos-er Michael Haydn—was resident in Salzburg, and the Mozarts certainly would have been his professional colleagues there. Perhaps Michael Haydn introduced his great brother Sepperl to Mozart in passing through Vienna, or even elsewhere.

At the same time the Baroque style was dying away, and the older structures were evolving into new designs; instrumental technology was changing too. (For the famous drudges who have striven to draw up the composer catalogues, the category of keyboard works has made them ache: again there was overlapping, and again things were more stable in Mozart's lifetime than in Haydn's.) The latter master, we are told, created about sixty "keyboard sonatas", so named since the bulk of them had to be played on the increasingly-archaic harpsichord, for the *pianoforte/fortepiano* was still being born. Mozart's sonatas total circa seventeen, and are listed as "Piano Music," presumably because by the younger man's death the builders had largely settled the harpsichord question. EN 5-10

One melancholy moment had yet to occur between the two great Austrian Classical friends: in 1790, the renowned Prince Nicholas I having died—and his successor having cut the lavish Esterhazy budget by dismissing most of the musicians—Haydn accepted an invitation to make an extended visit to England. In that era to make a winter crossing of the tumultuous English Channel was at best gambling one's life; the younger Mozart worried that his elderly friend would not survive the journey. ("Papa, I will never see you again!") As it happened, of course, it was the younger man who died at home in Austria at the end of 1791, and Haydn learned that tragic news while he was still in England. EN 5-11

• • •

Thus it was that Mozart could not be the founder of this new order. When "Wolferl" was four years of age, Haydn was almost thirty, and was having to produce entertainment for a Prince who played works daily himself; we are told on one occasion the Prince remarked to Haydn that of course the Kapellmeister was a better musician than the nobleman: it was simply his duty to be better! EN 5-12 Mozart was a great talent, however, and quickly chose the best elements from the new, evolving designs.

Hence an amazing circumstance occurred: before Haydn reached sixty, his great friend had died young, and having learned from Mozart's genius and insights, the older man used the period 1791-1805 (fifteen years!) to further refine the Classical style in his late symphonies, quartets, and oratorios - providing a set of prototypes, a set of aural structures perfect for Beethoven's and others' further exploitation. Haydn by 1809 had been given three-quarters of a century to draft the blue-prints for important musical architecture.

One sees this clearly in Mozart's and Haydn's rosters of key-board sonatas, as in their string quartets and some other *genres*. From 1770 or so to 1790, the two great friends were "riding a wave", and they knew it. Each relished the reinforcement he gave the other. They encouraged each other.

Undergraduates across the Western World are allowed to coalesce the two on exam answers; their names and styles be-come echoes: "Name one or more possible composer(s) of this recording." Easy answer: "Haydn or Mozart!" In fact, they are quite unlike: the typical Mozartian passage will be a double period of four four-bar units, while Haydn allows consecutive four-bar phrases only in variations forms, and other compara-tively rare cases. Haydn prefers to use "surprise" at every op-portunity. Igor Stravinsky once remarked to Marc Vignal: "Of all the musicians of his time, Haydn was the most cognizant, to my mind, that to be perfectly symmetrical means to be perfectly dead." EN 5-13

For recorded performance & commentary, please visit:

www.roberthamiltonpianist.com

Artistry: 3. Haydn, *Hob. XVI 48* & Mozart, *KV 333*

Mozart, Sonata KV 333, 2nd Mvt.

W. A. M. 333.

SONATE.

Andante con espressione.

J. Haydn.

№ 21.

7824

SONATE N.º 13
für das Pianoforte
von
W. A. MOZART.
Köch. Verz. N.º 333.

10(154)

W. A. M. 333.

Edition Peters. 7824

Recorded Voice-over remarks (printed version)

Hamilton

There are many who find little difference between the music of Haydn and Mozart. This is understandable, since both used what was a limited notational language during the time in which they lived. Once again, **Artistry** must dig beyond the notes to discover what is trying to be said. When we do this, we find very substantial differences! To summarize them, let us say that Mozart's output is characterized by a smooth, seldom interrupted flow, with beautiful melodic phrases of regular length. Haydn, on the other hand, is often irregular with sudden interruptions and changes in direction. It is most unfortunate that many performances of Haydn fail to recognize this, with the intended surprises unwisely rounded out through added dynamics and *ritardandi*. The result is that the music becomes totally predictable. In the matter of character, Haydn is the true forerunner of Beethoven. And because Haydn's erratic melodies are not at their best when performed with the natural flow of Mozart's, many listeners have come to consider him a second-class Mozart. This mischaracterization in performance is among the sadder chapters in music, including the incorrect approaches of many conductors, string quartets and pianists alike. Let's look at a couple of brief examples, to show the wide difference between these two composers.

First, here is the first theme of a typical Mozart slow

movement, the second of his *Sonata K. 333*. Listen for the singing and regular melodic line, whose attraction is its simple beauty and reliability....... Now compare part of a slow movement of Haydn, in this case the first movement of his *C major sonata, Hob. XVI: 48*. Listen to how the performance here exemplifies the irregularities and unpredictability of the journey....... And here is a bit of the *Mozart K. 333* first movement, again beautiful for its regularity and flowing melodic line.......

The finale of *Mozart's K.333* again moves along with charm and regularity....... Meanwhile Haydn's finale to the *C major sonata* thrives largely on the irregular and the unexpected. As a side note, I admit without apology to making the most of available possibilities to be un-predictable in this Haydn performance. I believe some performance exaggeration is helpful and even needed if we are ever to fully change perceptions, so that Haydn's music may be seen as "not Mozart".......

A Crucial Historical Sidelight: A Virtual Miracle

Much of what Beethoven, Chopin, and the nineteenth century treasured about the Viennese Classical Style came from syntheses of the two great Danubians, both of whom owed much to Johann Joseph Fux, the pedagogue of the *Gradus ad Parnassum*. [EN 5-14]

Everyone who seeks to understand the heritage of the Classical Style now owes a debt of gratitude to Fux, and to a Haydn biographer named Carl Ferdinand Pohl, who played his role more than a century after Haydn, Mozart, and Beethoven were all dead.

When Fux died in 1741 the nine-year-old Joseph Haydn probably sang for his funeral at *Stephansdom*. Fux's great pedagogical work, *Gradus ad Parnassum,* became Haydn's principal manual of counterpoint instruction, and Haydn had "devoured" the exercises in the text by the 1750s. (He was in good company: Sebastian Bach's own copy survives.) Haydn worked the problems, came back to them a few days later, and did them again. During his whole life, he continued to study Fux, and to annotate his copy. He seems to have made up copies of his own annotated *Gradus...* to distribute them to students (including Beethoven) and friends. Some such "condensed copies" still exist. Haydn's own complete and annotated version was, of course, extremely valuable, but it was lost in the chaos of World War II. [2]

Thus, the seminal work of Fux had bound together the Viennese Classical School through the dedicated scholarship of Carl Ferdinand Pohl! And in most practical terms, it had bound together the central figures of the School; that Mozart sought to emulate Haydn's op. 33 string quartets, published in 1781, with his own famous six from 1785, known today as Mozart's "Haydn Quartets", can hardly be doubted. On one occasion in that same year, Haydn uttered to Leopold Mozart what famously has become his own professional judgment: "Before God, and as an honest man, I tell you that your son is the greatest composer known to me in person or by reputation. He has

---

2 But "...Providentially Carl Ferdinand Pohl, the first major Haydn biographer, in what the great Alfred Mann himself felicitously calls "foresight dictated by scrupulous scholarship", had written out Haydn's annotations into Pohl's private copy of the *Gradus...,* and his copy survived the war! Mann believes "Haydn's annotated copy had gone through Mozart's hands." **EN 5-15**

taste, and, what is more, the greatest knowledge of composition." [EN 5-16] In his turn, Mozart is understood to have replied to the minor composer Kozeluch, who had criticized Haydn, that "Even if they melted us both together, there would still not be stuff enough to make a single Haydn!" [EN 5-17]

"Mutual admiration," indeed....

CHAPTER SIX

A Tale of Three
(Or Perhaps Four) Cities

Johannes Brahms: *Intermezzo in B Minor, op. 119, no. 1*

Demaree

Most of these great composers, as we have seen, developed and exhibited personality quirks. Perhaps of them the individual most damaged early on was Johannes Brahms: he apparently suffered a complicated, vividly-impacted youth that had lifelong effect on his nature. Circumstances of that un- usual childhood in Hamburg are said by many to have haunted his most intimate personal relationships for the remainder of his life.

Nor can his friends and acquaintances who have written in his era about these matters be concretely confirmed in Brahms' own writings, nor in the reminiscences of others. (Controversies about these facets of his private life, by the way, parallel closely the guesswork about Beethoven and his "Immortal Beloved.") Brahms' minute-to-minute and week-to-week behavior toward

others could be unpre-
dictable and inconsis-
tent—and his attitudes
toward his composing
and performing, his
loves, and all his plans
just as volatile.

• • •

For half a millen-
nium the vital trade
routes across the Baltic
region and along
Western Europe's
Atlantic coast were

Johannes Brahms portrait by James Foy, student
of the authors, c. 1975

Music room of Brahms, pastel on paper by Carl Müller, 1906

dominated by an impro-
vised commercial associa-
tion called "*Hanse*." Over
time, key municipalities
granted membership in this
powerful bloc were conceded the right to call themselves "Free and Hanseatic
Cities". One of the most
powerful of these—given
its wonderful river-mouth
harbor and advantageous
geographic location—even
today still denominates itself formally as the *Freie
und Hansestadt Hamburg.*
EN 6-1 Once a city becomes
a trading-port, it also becomes a habitat for shore
leave for sailors—with bars,
flophouses, gambling dens,
houses of prostitution, and
their ilk—and Hamburg's
sordid, sleazy "*Reeperbahn*"
neighborhood   remains
even today infamous and,
indeed, iconic as such
around the whole world (in
spite of all civic efforts to
the contrary). EN 6-2

DR. OTTO BÖHLER'S SCHATTENBILDER
18

JOHANNES BRAHMS

Johannes Brahms silhouette, Otto Böhler,
Vienna, Austria

Brahms' grave, Central Cemetery, Vienna

Ironically, the wealth of those traders of Hamburg slowly generated a broader populace in the city, as well; the region (recalling that Luther himself had written and published from nearby Wittenberg and Eisenach) was dominated after the Protestant Reformation by North German Lutherans who were both affluent and sanctimoniously fastidious. This climate of opulent taste had drawn, in intervening years, such men as Telemann, Mattheson, and Emanuel Bach (the latter imported from Frederick the Great's court, no less) to Hamburg. Hence one of the city's proudest traditions from the days of Handel to the present has been its fostering of grand opera. Its orchestras emerged from these same stimuli. Music—both elite and common—has flourished in this milieu: in the city, in its concert halls and on its wharves. [EN 6-3]

"Pop" groups performing there in the mid-twentieth century, for example, included the emerging Beatles. Born here in 1833, Brahms spent his youth primarily as a piano student, giving his debut recital at fifteen, and developing aggressively as a composer. To subsidize his family's income, he is thought to have played popular music in waterfront saloons. [EN 6-4] All his life, as a native of this cosmopolitan base, Johannes Brahms would interweave his music and attitudes with those of Hamburg, knowing well both its transience and its citizenry.

In his late teens he broke out of this local context, concertizing and visiting in north and central Germany; in just three life-changing years he met and visited with Joachim, Liszt himself, and—at age twenty—both the Schumanns, Robert and Clara. In the long run, his idol Robert's tragic illness and death were to involve Brahms in Leipzig, where the Schumanns' life together had begun in the famous legal fight with her father. Leipzig was

Clara's "once and future home." There she eventually would return to live and receive visitors after Robert's death.

Leipzig thus became the second of the primary cities in Brahms' life, as it had become the capital of pre-Imperial German music. Here, as we shall see in the next chapter, Bach had spent most of his career, and here Mendelssohn (see Chapter Eight) had resurrected him. Here was published the ranking music periodical: the *Neue Zeitschift für Musik* (which played a major role in juxtaposing Brahms and Wagner). Here stood both the historic *Gewandhaus,* with its still-famous Orchestra (which Brahms would conduct over a dozen times himself), ^{EN} ⁶⁻⁵ and the pre-Hitlerian *Mendelssohn Hochschule.*

Neither Hamburg nor Leipzig proved ideal for the young composer-conductor-pianist. The Leipzig premiere of Brahms' *D minor (First) Piano Concerto, op. 15,* for example, drew some hissing from the audience, and thus became an embarrassment to Frau Schumann and others. For a time, such controversies threatened his stature Europe-wide, but later he was to win over the Leipzig audiences.

In the meantime, having departed from one of the world's great mercantile centers, he looked for another home base, and found it in the most famous music site of all: Vienna. In warming to his music, the citizens of the great Habsburg imperial capital knew they were standing guard, extending again an unmatched roster: Brahms' predecessors had been Haydn, Mozart, Beethoven, Schubert, and a whole regiment of lesser figures. He moved into rooms near the splendid and unique *Karlskirche,* with its Trajanesque columns, to enjoy that view for the remainder of his life.

• • •

Brahms was unusually complicated as an individual, exhibiting important aspects of a "split personality." Direct contradictions abound in Brahms' life and attitudes. They seem to have begun to appear in his youth, and often reappeared in his later life. What were the most important of these in his work and associations?

His creative work exhibited characteristics his associates would define as both Classical and Romantic in an era when both "schools" were extant.[1]

He divided much of his life between commercial, low-German Hamburg and imperial Vienna—between money and nobility—with elitist, academic, snobbish Leipzig as an alternative, when he needed one.

As a result, he wrote both short forms (which tended to be Romantic: *lieder* and solo works for various instruments), and longer ones like symphonies, sonatas, concertos, and multi-movement chamber designs, perhaps because he thought only traditional longer forms would earn him attention from conductors, important artists, and critics.

Although he began composing with short forms and counterpoint exercises —as all young writers must— nevertheless he soon recognized that to be taken seriously he must create the traditional large forms; these occupied the majority of his mature years, as they had Haydn's, Mozart's, Beethoven's, and

---

1   Brahms in a notebook copied down "Form is the product of thousands of years of the greatest masters' efforts and something that each new generation cannot assimilate too quickly. It is but [a] delusion...to seek ...to achieve a perfection that already exists." EN 6-6

Wagner's. In Vienna, which was to be his home base for the remainder of his life, living in the great metropolis on the Danube would bring forth four symphonies, three more *concerti*, *Ein deutsches Requiem*, overtures, long rosters of chamber music and sonatas, plus major choral music, works for organ, and apparently a great many creations which he believed would not please critics, and which he thus destroyed.

At the end, however, he turned back substantially to the songs and short piano pieces that he had always loved; included were some of the greatest of his *Lieder*—the set of five in *op. 105*, beginning with *Wie melodien...*, for example—and much of his solo piano writing, including the *op. 119 Intermezzo* we study herein. (The *opp. 116-119* piano solo works were essentially his last, save for a set of organ preludes and the *Vier ernste Gesänge, op. 121*, the latter prompted by the approaching death of Clara Schumann.)

Even Brahms' close friends conceded—during his lifetime and after—that his were difficult mannerisms. He was often coarse and rude even to those (e.g. Clara Schumann, Joseph Joachim) to whom he was closest. And to those he believed wanted only to use him, he could be acidic.

Yet he was forgiving, too. Even after the hissing at his first piano concerto, by one count he returned to the *Gewandhaus* to conduct and/or perform *thirteen* times. Thus, he could be generous, and even loving, especially to artists he admired, and children. In the closing years of his life an unusually talented young contralto named Alice Barbi departed from Vienna to marry an Italian nobleman, and scheduled a farewell recital of Brahms' songs. The waiting audience were amazed to see her float onstage that evening, followed by her shambling, bear-like pianist for the concert—Brahms himself! We are told he had gone by surprise to her dressing room a few minutes earlier, asking for the "privilege" of accompanying her himself that evening. He did so before an astonished audience. EN 6-7

Almost certainly Brahms' sexual proclivities—his avoidance of marriage to any of the women he idolized: Clara Schumann (after Robert's death), Agathe von Siebold, Elizabeth von Herzogenberg, *née* von Stockhausen, or others, and his frequenting of prostitutes (common public gossip, especially in Vienna) stemmed from his days as a good-looking young man sexually mistreated on the Hamburg docks, as did his ambivalence toward women—so-called "good girls" (his Madonna-like mother and apparently, the widowed Clara) versus "bad girls" (the "sailors' girls" in Hamburg and the prostitutes he was generally said to have visited regularly in Vienna).[2] And then there is the published personal testimony of the great Vienna critic Max Graf, who listened as Brahms—at the behest of a "lady" who spoke quite familiarly to the great man—played popular music for a long time on a piano in a *Bierstube,* performing from memory songs and waltzes that would have been familiar to clientele on the docks in Hamburg. EN 6-8

And ultimately there was his quandary about religion: born a North German Protestant and buried from the only Protestant church in the old *Innere Stadt* of Vienna, he nevertheless treasured all the symbolism in the *Karlskirche* just outside his *Karlsgasse* window. He was able authoritatively to cite Luther's

---

2   Note that some current-day scholarship argues young Johannes could not have played music on the docks, for there were city ordinances against child labor. Of course, city ordinances existed in other places and generations too, and were simply ignored! Remember Al Capone?

translations of the two Testaments in the *Deutches Requiem,* but he never referred to Jesus Christ by name, and his protégé, Dvorak, said of him regretfully: "He believes in nothing!" ^{EN 6-9} Yet in the movement he had inserted last into the *Requiem,* set as an afterthought, a soprano soloist's voice sings repeatedly and lingeringly above the choir "I will see you again;" *wiederseh'n.., wiederseh'n.., wiederseh'n.* Perhaps the death of his mother four years earlier made him wish to be a believer; the same ambivalence about religion appears in other works, but about a reunion with his Madonna mother he would brook no doubt.

What is more, near the end of his life, as his beloved Clara Wieck Schumann lay dying, he created the *Vier ernste Gesänge, op. 121,* the last of which ends with the famed passages from *Ecclesiastes* addressing Death and Saint Paul's lines from First Corinthians in which "Love abideth." He would not attend a public performance of these as long as he lived. ^{EN 6-10}

Regarding his mother and Clara, he was unwilling to be an agnostic. Did he now hope for rebirth himself? One can only speculate: was the aging Brahms envisioning for himself reunions with his earthly loves in a fourth great home—Augustine of Hippo's *City of God*—far beyond Hamburg, Leipzig, and Vienna?

"When we speak about Brahms's music…we are forced to resort to abstractions: this theme, this rhythm, this design…. His elusiveness of person and voice and 'meaning' is close to the essential mystery of music itself." ^{EN 6-11}

The structure of *op. 119, no. 1*—the first of a set of four short forms—is a straight-forward ternary. The final section of *no. 1* is a standard variant of the opening. There are many recordings by famous artists—Serkin, Perahia, Gould, Ax, etc.—of *op. 119, no.1*, and they vary greatly, especially in *tempi*. These artists found justifications for **Intuition**.

<u>For recorded performance & commentary, please visit:</u>
www.roberthamiltonpianist.com
Artistry: 4. Brahms, *Intermezzo, Op. 119 #1*

Klavierstücke.

Intermezzo.

Adagio.   Op. 119 № 1. *(1893.)*

Recorded Voice-over remarks (printed version)

Hamilton

The music of Johannes Brahms presents a variety of performance possibilities and questions: as, for example, how much to move forward or hold back, whether to perform thickly or with an elegant textural buoyancy, even the struggle of a sometimes-tortured counterpoint. Some performances will reveal a struggle within the music, while other worthy approaches make the decision to simply go one way or the other. To demonstrate some of the wide array of choices before the **Artist**, I will present the opening phrases of his 1st *Intermezzo* from *Opus 119,* in four differing versions. Noticeable variants will include tempo and dynamics, but repeated hearings will reveal a lot of subtle changes involving *rubato*, stress points, voicing, articulation and sound coloring. All of this of course affects the carried message of the music. And once again, note that little of what is going on in these performances is offered as directions in the printed score.......

Now to consider the overall message and matters of structural balance, let's follow this last version through its completed four-minute journey. Note the interplay with the written rhythm, which, besides clarifying phrase meanings, embodies some of the natural push and pull of the Brahms personality. While large expressive liberties will be taken, they will be interlaced with moments of rhythmic exactness, and we will never abandon a sense of direction or destination. This is, of course, just one possible **interpretation**, and I have chosen to move far away from a literal translation of the score. While some renditions, mine and others', will go this far, some will not.......

• • •

In summary, Brahms' "direct contradictions" offer us much freedom to interpret; indeed, they urge us to do so.

Obviously, Brahms was not the same man every day. And obviously he would not have shaped a single phrase the same way, or chosen exactly the same tempo, or committed to the same sequence of attacks day after day. Nor is it a composer's purpose to require a slavish sameness of colleagues. (The reader already will have experienced a variety of expressions of the famous first four notes of the "Beethoven Fifth.")

CHAPTER SEVEN
The Master of Us All

Johann Sebastian Bach: *WTC II,*
Prelude and Fugue in E Major

Demaree

Before the colossus that is Johann Sebastian Bach one stands silent; then the memories of the music he has written sound in the ear, and the almost unfathomable genius comes to life again. The achievement was so vast, the talent so formidable, and the conceptions so profound, that only the chords, the rhythms, the counterpoint, and the melodies themselves can enable us to reach the man behind them.

To read about his life, and to guess the rest (the diffidence of the burghers, the shallowness of the patrons, the squalling children, the lawsuits, and everything else common and trivial) explains so little. To learn what people of his own time said about him—comparing him more or less unfavorably to Telemann, or even to others whose names are recalled now only because of their proximity to Bach's career—is to wonder from what blindness we of this modern age suffer, and what talents of today go unseen and unheard.

To approach the music of Sebastian Bach is a labor of love and respect for the megalith whose works we have been performing for well over three centuries. The debt for all the beauty, the power, the serenity, and, most of all, the reassurance, is too great to be paid.

Bach did not intend that we purchase his music: it was not created to be sold at public concerts and in music shops. He did not write it for us. Rather, he dedicated it, and just so do we offer up our limited, worldly talents in studying its performance, not in payment to Bach for his music, but in gratitude for his life. In doing so, we rejoice in Art that was, and is, and ever shall be. Amen. [EN 7-1]

Engraving of a portrait of J.S. Bach by August Weger, c. 1870

Portrait of J.S. Bach seated at the organ, artist unknown, 1725

•••

In early 1685 the townspeople of the substantial village of Eisenach (on the south flank of the historic Wartburg Castle's *Berg*, roughly fifty miles from Weimar) would have regarded the unfolding history of the area as largely accomplished. There had been already at least three decisive moments: (1) the arrival of the Roman legions in the forested lands of what we would now call North Central Germany, (2) the subsequent overpowering of those Imperial forces, foreshadowing the evolution of the medieval feudal states of Thüringia and its emerging neighbors, and (3) the hijacking into asylum of Martin Luther by the Landgraf/Elector Frederick III during the crucial year of 1521; over the next couple of decades,

Grave of J.S. Bach, Thomaskirche, Leipzig, Germany

BACH MONUMENT IN MARKET-PLACE AT EISENACH.

Bach monument in Market-Place at Eisenach

Luther marshalled with words the Protestant revolutionaries, thereby consolidating and formalizing in the Wartburg what would become both the "Lutheran" Church and the German language itself!

It was not just the language of German that was changing—stabilizing—but the alphabet of music itself. In the West the struggle to agree on tuning and temperament went back to Ancient Greece: since the time of Pythagoras various tuning systems had been contrived over two-and-a-half millennia, but each theoretical model collapsed when confronted with two basic problems: (1) how to combine ensembles of fixed-pitch instruments (particularly keyboards) with variable-pitch producers (voices, winds, strings, etc.) without ugly simultaneities, and (2) how to "modulate" music between keys without creating "wolf tones" and similar distractions. From the time of Pythagoras to the present, literally hundreds of scholars and scientists (Paul Hindemith, for a recent case) have tried and failed to resolve the problem. The fixed-pitch instruments appear to have won, at least for the moment. [EN 7-2]

In the time of Sebastian Bach, the search for a solution to this age-old temperament enigma arrived at an intermediate system known as "well-tempered tuning." Bach, recognized as a keyboard **Artist** himself, of course, favored this compromise and demonstrated its flexibility in an extensive composition of two volumes, each with twenty-four prelude-and-fugue pairs, that he called the Well-Tempered Clavier (*Das Wohltempierte Clavier*). [EN 7-3] Out of this vast catalog we shall extract and examine from *WTC II* the *Fugue in E Major*.[1]

The tower of works he constructed—vocal and instrumental, solo, chamber, and large ensemble, religious and secular, short and long, passions in lieu of operas, Italian and French styles, as well as his native German media—is unmatched. One must come to the great question sooner or later: How did he manage this constant flow (along with his tutorial, conductorial, and administrative daily chores) for decades?

The foundation stone on which this tower rests is counterpoint. From that base each of his structures rises. Just as the spires of sixteenth-century Renaissance choral music were assembled out of cascades of point-of-imitation contrapuntal voicing, alternating with passages of homophony, so the eighteenth-century High Baroque towers would be constructed of assemblages of canonic and fugal conglomerates, especially the quasi-mathematical "invertible counterpoint", and combinations thereof ("canonic fugues," for example), all in the spirit, especially in Bach, of making the textures more complex in a competition against oneself—which became Bach's lifelong challenge.

---

1 Note that since Mendelssohn's "rediscovery" of him through the *St. Matthew Passion*, Bach has generally been thought of in the West as a "church musician," given the *St. John,* [EN 7-4] all the church cantatas, the organ preludes, the Magnificats, the Mass in B Minor, the *Christmas Oratorio*, and so much more; yet all these ignore *The Art of the Fugue, The Musical Offering, the Brandenburg Concerti,* the *"Coffee" Cantata*, the *WTC I and II*, the *Chromatic Fantasy and Fugue*, the *Goldberg Variations*, the *Italian Concerto,* the six stunning Cello Suites, the magnificent double (violin) *Concerto in D Minor*, and so many other preeminent works. Bach's fame rests on music both *sacra* and *profana*. We know Bach was devout, but he was not unequivocally a church musician, just as Haydn (two generations later) was not primarily a symphonist, as has been generally said of him. As the word "Thuringer" now refers to either a dweller in the Eisenach area, or a plump type of German sausage, so Sebastian Bach wrote both sacred and secular music.

Examine such early scores as the *Fifteen Inventions* (written in the 1720s for Bach's eldest son Wilhelm Friedemann). The first, in C major, begins with an almost monolithic subject twelve notes long, set immediately in counterpoint against nine-, eight-, and four-note variants of the opening motif. All this material is invertible, of course, and the number of measures Bach actually had to "compose" is thereby reduced substantially.

The same can be seen in the other Inventions. Both *No. 4, D minor,* and *No. 8, F major,* are masterful in their construction. In the first of these the original two-bar subject appears every two or three measures for the duration of the work; in the other, the composer shows us another of his time-saving procedures: if the first twelve measures in F major will modulate to the dominant by measure 12, then he need not spend his time getting back "home." The invertible counterpoint at bar 26 will carry us back to the dominant of B-flat by the last chord. Thus, we see the first stage in building his "towers," for here in the Inventions the master has shown us elementary and canonic counterpoint in completed blocs, yet he has composed only a few original measures in each segment. To extend a work he need only add further such components, controlling the overall tonic and the meter as he goes.

One of the greatest of Bach's early choral works, the "Sixth Motet," BWV 230, *Lobet den Herrn alle Heiden,* can instruct us further: here we begin in C major (in 4/4) with a sprawling four-voice fugue, and several fugal developments, ending with a reprise of the original subject. Next comes the contrast of a relatively homophonic section, followed by a third distinct unit, featuring long sustained pitches in each voice in turn, and proceeding to an apparent "final" cadence in the governing 4/4

C major. Now comes a surprising shift to a brilliant and joyful triple-meter "Alleluia" which (remaining in C major and reminding one of the codas of a Tomás Luis de Victoria motet) ends the work. Thus, we have four component segments, each built up out of contrapuntal procedures, ultimately comprising an entire work—a masterwork—that exemplifies Bach's conceiving of whole structures.

And yet this is not the ultimate layer! Bach never wrote an opera, although he certainly was capable of doing so. He did create "large forms" one structural level higher: the *Goldberg Variations*, the *St. Matthew Passion*, the *Mass in B Minor*, the *Brandenburg Concerti*, and (among all the others) the *WTC I and II* we are about to approach.

The WTC is represented herein by the Ninth *Praeludium/ Fuga* from Volume II. Both are in E major, the *Praeludium* in triple meter, and the *Fuga* in either duple or 4/2.[2] The *Praeludium* is a traditional binary form, modulating to the dominant; continuing there after the repeat, it quickly wanders afield tonally, and then returns to E major with fifteen measures to go. The entire movement relies on figuration and invertible counterpoint.

The architecture of the E major *Fuga IX* is traditional, and grand. The subject first appears in tonic, and three more rising statements—BTAS, on tonic, dominant, tonic, and dominant—form a six-measure Exposition I. A two-measure episode postpones the next exposition (also in E, as will be the final one after C-sharp), and other episodes.

---

2 Some historic editions mark the one, others the other. Essentially no markings but the pitches and rhythms can be trusted as Bach's own. Beyond even that, at the bottom margin of modern editions whole paragraphs report pitches altered from even such as Simrock.

For recorded performance & commentary, please visit:

www.roberthamiltonpianist.com

Artistry: 5. Bach, *Fugue in E Major, WTC II #9*

FUGA IX.

B.W. XIV.

B.W. XIV.

Recorded Voice-over remarks (printed version)

Hamilton

The music of J.S. Bach presents unique problems for the pianist, who is of course rendering a transcribed version of music written for earlier keyboard instruments. At the center are the forty-eight preludes and fugues of the two volumes of the *Well-Tempered Clavier*. It should be borne in mind that, while most early-instrument performances today are done on the harpsichord, the work was also meant for clavichord, a very low-volume instrument which nonetheless could play with expressive nuance and was, in this respect, superior to the harpsichord. Playing a fugue on the modern piano both permits and invites expressive rendering, though the performer should take care not to get overly carried away. Nor, on the other hand, should we try to strip the modern instrument of its inherent nature by playing with as little nuance as possible in an attempt to imitate the harpsichord. Rhythmic freedom is another considered walk between the extremes of absolute unbending strictness, and total freedom without boundaries. The bottom line: there are many beauties to be expressed in a Bach fugue, as well as the spiritual message. Performances must be inspirational, not just correct. But we must also respect the period from which it came. Artists will naturally differ on the appropriate middle ground. Here is one example of my approach, by way of the *E-major Fugue* of the 2nd book of the *WTC*.......

On the 31st of March (O.S.) in 1685, what burgher in Eisenach would have judged that a baby boy born that day to a local family would prove as great an historical figure as Caesar Augustus, the guerilla leader Arminius ("Herman, the German"), or the Elector Frederick? We all live lives studded with unpredictable miracles. Sebastian Bach was such a miracle.

CHAPTER EIGHT
The Young Genius

Felix Mendelssohn-Bartholdy, *Variations Sérieuses, op. 54*

Demaree

Name a child prodigy—or two—or three.... (They're not really rare.) Such is not our primary goal in this study, of course, for **Artistry** can be assessed and encouraged at any age, any stage of development. The real goal for all great musicians—teachers, students, famous performers—is Artistry. The media, however, love photo-journalism that showcases child stars: Artur Rubinstein played his debut at age 10, with Brahms's friend Joseph Joachim conducting, but in his '80s—still playing two piano *concerti* on one program with the *Concertgebouw*—Rubinstein characterized himself to a television interviewer ^{EN 8-1} as "the most fortunate of men because all my life I have loved music!" After some seventy-five years, he cared little that he had been a child prodigy. He probably did recall with pride, though, that he had played under Joachim, who was a great **Artist**. So...

Name a prodigy, or two, or three, or dozens. Many, of course, have been fakes, like carnival freaks or anomalies. Even Beethoven's father in Bonn was said to have trimmed a couple of early months off his son's age. The famous figure most often described as a true child prodigy these days is undoubtedly Mozart, yet that

Felix Mendelssohn Bartholdy, Lithograph by Friedrich Jentzen, 1837

cliché too, is media-driven, and uninformed. By any fair measure Schubert's youthful *Lieder* (he wrote *Erl-König* at eighteen,

Das Mendelssohn'sche Haus in der Leipziger Strasse in Berlin.
Palais Groeben, Mendelssohn residence in Berlin, Leipziger Strasse, 1900

for example) are more memorable and successful today than Mozart's teenage writings. [EN 8-2] So, list Mozart, Schubert, Bernstein, Rubinstein, Michael Jackson, Olde King Cole, and all the hundreds of Merrie Younge Soules, and what do you have? For ninety-five per cent of them, memories of glittering lights and condescending adults. The years pass into ennui for the performer after the debuts are over and

Reconstructed Mendelssohn monument near Leipzig's Thomaskirche, dedicated in 2008

Drawing of Thomaskirche by Felix Mendelssohn, c. 1843

the lights dim, for only Artistry will justify study and labor through the decades.

Name a child prodigy.... How about Felix Mendelssohn?

That young man by his teens had shown himself to be prodigious as both composer and performer (one who played his debut at age nine)—a prodigy fully as remarkable as the already-legendary Mozart and Schubert. As a pianist and a composer his elder sister Fanny was talented as well, and both of these affluent children became sensations.

• • •

Members of a notable German-Jewish family, born into real opulence as grandchildren of the highly-esteemed philosopher Moses Mendelssohn, Fanny and Felix grew to maturity facing two overwhelming prejudices: (1) the wealthy are always envied, if not always hated, and (2) anti-Semitism was endemic in German society. (Fanny confronted a third such bias: as a *female* pianist/composer/ conductor, she broke new ground a full century before the talented American "Mrs. H. H. Beach" could be recognized as "Amy Beach"—and a generation before "Frau Robert Schumann" could become "Clara Wieck Schumann.")

As to wealth, the Mendelssohn family controlled a Berlin banking house powerful all over Europe, and that wealth enabled both Fanny and Felix to grow up with prestigious tutelage and facility in a range of languages and media. (As an example, study the quality of Felix's watercolors.) EN 8-3 Both these children were well taught, gracious, and aristocratic.

As to religion, politically the family was split. One branch continued as traditional Jews. However, Felix was apparently baptized in secret at age seven, when his branch of the relatives added the hyphenation "Bartholdy" as a protective last name. ^{EN 8-4}

In his childhood years in Berlin, he indeed played his debut performance at age nine, wrote a unique double string quartet, and composed a remarkably mature *Overture for A Midsummer Night's Dream* (Shakespeare). Both works are still much played; by his late teens, he had been introduced to and had greatly interested Goethe and Cherubini. He became widely known.[1]

• • •

For the West this was a cosmopolitan age, and particularly an era for the formation of great music organizations: the *Wiener Philharmoniker* and the Metropolitan Opera (both 1842), the *Berlin Philharmoniker* (1882), and the *Royal Concertgebouw Orchestra* (1888). Earlier the historically conservative city of Leipzig had assembled its *Gewandhaus Orchester*—traditionally the forerunner of the modern player-managed symphony orchestra—out of various mid-to-late-eighteenth-century concert enterprises. Thus, it was a sign of great change when Leipzig in 1835 named the twenty-six-year-old Felix Mendelssohn conductor of its famous old *Gewandhaus Orchester*. His revival at

---

1 Another example of his careful fostering and personal discipline: although Berlioz is often judged to be the renowned master of orchestration of this period, Mendelssohn also became expert in this discipline. (It has been said that, had he miscalculated the voicing of the famous repeated eighth-note chords that constitute the opening of his "Italian Symphony", the passage would have sounded "like a crazy chickenyard.") As a master of orchestration, he seems to have become the equal of Berlioz and Rimsky-Korsakov.

age twenty in Berlin in 1829 of the *St. Matthew Passion,* which had lain unperformed for almost exactly a century since its premiere, had led to an opportunity to repeat the monumental work in its birthplace, Leipzig itself. His inheritance of the podium of the *Gewandhaus* was influenced at least in part by his restoration of the memory of that city's "patron saint."

Moreover, Mendelssohn's influence and post of power enabled him to create another music institution, initially known as the "Conservatorium," but later designated the "Mendelssohn Academy". Thus "the young genius" took a commanding role in Leipzig in the 1830s, at just the mid-point of his life. His stewardship of *Gewandhaus* programing was far-sighted; his influence would draw as guest artists and composers each of the Schumanns, and in the next generation Brahms (both as conductor and pianist), Wagner, and Liszt.

• • •

The definitive year 1831 began just the second half of Mendelssohn's brief life. Major and mature compositions became the focus of his work (although to many they may now seem somewhat less fresh and imaginative than that string octet and *Midsummer Night's Dream* overture written in his teens). 1831 was a landmark year in many ways: Darwin sailed on the *Beagle,* Karl von Clausewitz—Prussian soldier and strategist—died, leaving *Vom Krieg* (On War) to influence twentieth-century military planning. In music, Chopin left Poland for Paris, [EN 8-5] Brahms' colleague-to-be Joseph Joachim was born, and Pleyel died. The preferences and advantages of wealth and fine tutelage had made it natural that young Felix would honor

Baroque and Classical traditions in music, and would approach and welcome the forms and textures around him.

Haydn had died at the peak of his fame the year Mendelssohn was born; Beethoven had yet eighteen years to work. Like any standard musical apprentice of that era, young Felix undertook careful study of the forms and the crafts of sonata design and counterpoint. Compared to the late nineteenth century, his major works were formally conservative, but lyrical.

A new European audience was evolving. It was listening not only to Baroque choral works and keyboard counterpoint, but also to the solo voice-and-piano settings of Schubert, Schumann, and especially the young poets and singers. Melody became the focal parameter of the new music of the time, from the salon-style concerts of new Schubert *Lieder* to the opera houses that celebrated Wagner's "endless melodies." (Looking back from Broadway, and over a century of sentimental songs, it can seem that music was always organized thus, but compare the *WTC* to *South Pacific* to clear the air!)

In 1842, five years before he died suddenly, Mendelssohn wrote: "People often complain that music is too ambiguous. Everyone understands words, of course, but listeners do not know what they should think when they hear music. With me," he said, 'it is exactly the opposite... [individual words] ...seem to me so ambiguous and vague, so easily misunderstood in comparison to genuine music... [T]he thoughts it does express are conveyed more clearly and fully than they would be by words." EN 8-6

One of Mendelssohn's decisions out of this viewpoint caught the cultural moment and froze it in time. Rather than writing another *Winterreise* or *Schwanengesang*, he began not a cycle, but a whole genre of "Songs Without Words" *(Lieder ohne Worten)*. Ranging over almost a hundred opus numbers, these individual works became extremely popular (especially among the broader population), and thus shaped the audience to come. In the "century of *Lieder"* his *Lieder ohne Worten* were widely played by both lay- and professional pianists (and still are). "Mendelssohn societies" formed around the Western world; *Elijah* and *St. Paul* restored the oratorio design to the stature it had in the time of Handel *(Messiah)* and Haydn *(Die Schöpfung)*. Among Mendelssohn's greatest scores are the *"Italian" Symphony (#3)* and his final major work, the much-beloved *Violin Concerto in E minor, op. 64.* (Note the evolving but Classical forms in the three movements of this traditional concerto design.)

The *Variations Sérieuses, op. 54*, written three years earlier, is a solo work, of course, not a concerto, yet it recalls that *op. 64* large form in its Classical style and restraint.

For recorded performance & commentary, please visit:
www.roberthamiltonpianist.com
Artistry: 6. Mendelssohn, *Variations Sérieuses, op. 54*

VARIATIONS SERIEUSES

Edited by Alfred A. Butler

From the CENTURY LIBRARY of MUSIC
Edited by Ignace J. Paderewski

F. MENDELSSOHN
Op. 54

Copyright 1900, by The University Society, Inc.

834-17-CB

VI

6-1

Recorded Voice-over remarks (printed version)

Hamilton

Using the theme of Mendelssohn's *Variations Sérieuses,* I would like to show the influence which tempo selection has upon the artistic image of a piece. The theme's presentation is crucial to initiating a message for this entire piece of seventeen variations plus coda. Mendelssohn gives the marking of *"Andante sostenuto"*. *'Andante'* directs us to play at a walking pace, while *'sostenuto'* (meaning sustained or prolonged) implies the stretching out of individual tones. These words might seem to be in conflict, and we must make a decision about how much to press forward—to create the walking movement—and how much to stretch (or to hold back) some individual tones. Each pianist must also determine the overall speed that will work best for accommodating the two goals. In trials, we may find that the acceptable tempo range is actually quite wide. I will present four options: two on the faster side, then two that are slower. The first option represents a more straightforward approach. The second, while taken at nearly the same tempo, is more free, taking some liberty with the time elements. The third and fourth options demonstrate the increasing effectiveness of tempo slowness to create *sostenuto*. Please note, however, that even the last and slowest version maintains Mendelssohn's quarter note pulse and does not plod along with an inappropriate eighth-note pulse that could become static and vertical. In playing at slower tempi, it is very important to return to tempo each time we employ a sustaining *rubato*. From the fastest version here to the slowest, there is a substantial difference of seventeen seconds, from forty-three seconds all the way up to sixty! Please note the wide effects of tempo selection on the message and artistic image of the work. As a side note, it is also important in this theme to use careful voicing, keeping each of the parts flowing in a meaningful line and at the appropriate dynamic levels.......

There was much confusion and no little unfairness in the West's view of Mendelssohn after World War II. The Nazis had hewn down his statues, renamed the "Conservatorium," and scrubbed his name off buildings and plaques, but Hitler's lackeys also destroyed documents and concert programs. Scholars will never again see or search through many (perhaps most) of these papers. That did not happen to the records of other great German composers. For example, modern scholars know that the splendid Clara Wieck Schumann—herself a "star pianist," and the widow of Robert Schumann—performed under Mendelssohn's baton at least twenty-one times. Did she not play these *Variations Sérieuses* sometime in recital? What did she have to say about the work? Much of this destructive sacrilege was pure "racial" malevolence, a broad attempt to deny that a remarkable individual ever existed.

Felix Mendelssohn-Bartholdy was one of the very greatest of composers, but conservative in style (as others have been). We all may have lost much.

CHAPTER NINE

The Dane

Carl August Nielsen: *Chaconne, op. 32*

Demaree

The present authors recall a Swedish-born colleague who— at the end of long days of adjudicating student pianists' semester hearings— would invariably ask, a bit petulantly, "Where was all the Scandinavian repertoire today?" Indeed, there likely had been none proffered. Grieg and Sibelius could have been identified by faculty and some students (a few would have known also of Gade and Nielsen), but the day had been dominated by the usual Germans, French, Russians, and even occasional Americans, Spanish, Poles, Hungarians, and Czechs. The broad expanses of the Northland were supposed to be only the province of yodeling, and of the Grieg Concerto.

So we begin this chapter with a bit of an apology. We must give our late colleague full credit for knowing a considerable swath of literature that many did not at that time (and that we have since grown to value, play, and record). The six Nielsen symphonies alone are a vigorous and idiomatic contribution to surely the most important genre since the Viennese Classicists; but one is reduced to imagining famous conductors able to plead only ignorance of these works. Yet Nielsen's Fourth (*The Inextinguishable*), for example, would hold its own against most of the very best standard symphonic repertoire. His volumi-

Carl Nielsen portrait photo, c. 1908

nous vocal literature is little sung, particularly, of course, because of the inconvenient fact that most singers (not including

Carl Nielsen home

the late, great Jussi Björling, who was fluent in both Swedish songs and *La Bohème*) have not been taught Scandinavian diction in studios.

• • •

Management of continuity—what some call "line" or "flow"—is a concern of composers that spans the centuries. A variety of systems have had their turns; some have been and remain ubiquitous, and others have functioned (perhaps even dominated) for only a few decades. Contrapuntal architectures have been devised for use in almost every genre since at least Compostela, extending through *organum* and the Netherlandians to the Gabrielis and the heights of the Venetian style; past Monteverdi and Fux to the High Baroque of Sebastian

Carl Nielsen's grave, sculpture by Anne Marie Carl Nielsen

Bach and Handel, and from the last scene of *Tristan und Isolde* to the *Concerto for Orchestra* and beyond.

Not every apparent system has lasted. Two extreme mechanisms, inherently complex, the late-fourteenth-century School of Mannerism and the recent short-lived Serialism Movement (which seemed in the 1970s apt to sweep all before it), have both in their times withered and left precious few descendants.

Newly-invented (composed) music probably began as (1) simple, repetitive chants and (2) so-called "through-composed" works (that is, whole *opera* with no repetition). The former are encountered principally on playgrounds and in stadia, the latter seem practical only for short pieces. It appears clearly-perceivable forms are as requisite to concert listeners as they are to tourists viewing city architecture. "Through-composed" works lacked sufficient continuity, and the concept has generally failed.

Nevertheless, composers have sought a greater variety of organizing principles over the centuries. Many have been conceived and attempted but, though found effective in particular circumstances, have proven too idiosyncratic to be broadly usable: Scriabin's ways of linking music and colors, for example; various mixed media (accompanied narration, as with Brahms' *Magalone Lieder* and Copland's *Lincoln Portrait*, or Prokofiev's *Peter and the Wolf*); linkages of tales with song cycles or other program music settings (as with *Winterreise*); or, in a broader context, "symphonic tone poems" and similar program music itself (including background stories like *Death and Transfiguration*).

Early polyphony set (that is, balanced) pre-existent chant (the "tenor") against one or more newly-composed contrapuntal voices, at first freely, and gradually in more controlled ways (especially imitatively) through "points of imitation" or canonic devices, including "rounds" and "fugal procedures." One of these evolving devices, in rather a return to using a "tenor"-like foundation for the other voices, implied the more-or-less continuous repetition of a melodic/rhythmic (or, later, harmonic) fragment throughout the passage or movement. Generally in the lowest voice, this mechanism was known variously by such terms as "ground bass" or "*basso ostinato.*"

Two terms became famously confused: "*Chaconne*" (originally a melodic ostinato), and "*passacaglia*" (with, instead, an established harmonic pattern) have been used interchangeably by contemporaneous composers. Sebastian Bach wrote his famous D minor solo violin *Chaconne* (*ciaccona*); Brahms' eight-chord harmonic succession that opens and underlays the Finale of the *Symphony No. 4 in E minor, op. 98,* has been traditionally spoken of as a *passacaglia,* but Brahms himself called it a *chaconne.*[1]

• • •

The fountain of Scandinavian concert music started flowing essentially with Niels Gade, who began to perform and compose in Copenhagen in the 1830s. He was a typical transitional figure,

---

1 What to do? Brahms' most recent biographer deals with this confusion as part of a five-page analysis of this single movement, calling the *passacaglia* "a similar genre to *chaconne*" [EN 9-1] and links this same movement to Brahms' farewell to Clara Schumann in the *Vier ernste Gesänge.* This sidestep is also the choice of the man who is probably the best authority on the whole controversy; he dodges it: "Understanding of the *passacaglia* and *chaconne* can therefore be greatly facilitated by using those terms only for pieces so designated by their composers." [EN 9-2] (Those readers familiar with Jazz styles will tend toward *C- Jam Blues* as a parallel.)

studying with a local teacher, and writing songs to German texts. His early orchestral writing drew attention, and he had the courage to send his new symphony to Mendelssohn himself in all-important Leipzig, where the great young man performed the work with the *Gewandhaus Orchester*. Invited to Leipzig, Gade conducted the *Orchester* himself, and—after this auspicious beginning there—inherited that podium on Mendelssohn's early death. A generation later a young pianist, one Edward Grieg (a contact of the famous Norse violinist Ole Bull), followed Gade to Leipzig. He studied with Gade and Moscheles. Grieg became a cosmopolitan European; although his piano writing was best-known worldwide, his chamber music and orchestral catalog remain popular.

The most portentous of the Scandinavians, thus far, seems to have been the Finn, Jean Sibelius, born a contemporary of Nielsen in the next generation after Grieg. Each of these — Gade, Grieg, Sibelius, and Nielsen—represented to an extent the musical idiom of his motherland (Sibelius perhaps most of all, because of the patriotic passion in his homeland at the time his *Finlandia* "anthem" came to signify the Finns' stand against the Red Army and the Nazis in the 1940s). Sibelius' focus on symphonies and concerti elevated his repute quickly, too.

· · ·

Carl (August) Nielsen himself was born on Funen (Danish: Fyn), a more-or-less pastoral island cramped between Jutland (the mainland), Zeeland (the island site of Copenhagen), and the nest of surrounding Danish islets. Although it is now dominated by the city of Odense, with its population in six figures,

Funen in the mid-nineteenth century was quite rural, and that focused young Carl on nature all his life. He was born there in 1865 to a farm family, a family defined as "poor" by biographer Torben Schousboe. [EN 9-3] Nielsen's father was apparently a rather capable "country" violinist and cornetist, who headed a local, popular "dance band." To this point young Carl was progressing through a childhood combining Joseph Haydn's "kitchen-pot percussion exploration" with Brahms' paternal guidance and management. His 1927 (age sixty-two) autobiography *Min fynske barndom* reminisces about and emphasizes the simplicity and natural beauties around him. [EN 9-4]

At age fourteen he was playing brass instruments in a military band in Odense. [EN 9-5] In the 1880s he studied piano and violin in Copenhagen, and gained a position as a second violinist in the royal chapel. [EN 9-6]

Next began his primary devotion to composition, which would prove as great a source of pride to the Danes (at the least) as Grieg's works are to the Norse. The present authors deduce at least five reasons Nielsen's music failed to "break through" in the forty years he had left for writing after 1890: (1) the Danish language and typography were/are obscure to most Westerners, (2) Nielsen did not foster a flamboyant image for himself, as did Strauss, Schoenberg, Webern, Stravinsky, and others, (3) Copenhagen lacked the "media focus" of Berlin, Paris, Vienna, New York, London, and other "world capitals," (4) radio and recording companies had not yet become the markets they would constitute in the middle of the twentieth century, and (5) the extent to which serial composers would give the media excuses for sensationalizing them was unforeseen by and discouraging to younger and older musicians world-wide.

It is the present authors' belief that two generations in the West have already "missed the boat" on Nielsen's six symphonies (especially *Nos. 4, 5, and 6),* the overture *Helios,* the songs, and certain chamber music. Virtually everything dated 1890 or later should be heard. Among these is, without a doubt, the splendid *Chaconne, op. 32.*

For recorded performance & commentary, please visit:
www.roberthamiltonpianist.com
Artistry: 7. Nielsen, *Chaconne, op. 32*

Chaconne
Op. 32

Carl Nielsen

16748

16743

(The entire score is printed on the website)

Recorded Voice-over remarks (printed version)

Hamilton

Danish composer Carl Nielsen composed a fine body of piano works that are, unfortunately, largely neglected. His *Chaconne, Opus 32,* provides a nicely concise opportunity to consider how a well-designed theme and variations should unfold seamlessly to create one satisfying whole. Too often, in performances of variation sets from any of the musical periods, listeners are subjected to unnecessary and excessive contrasts that fail to meet the critical task of conveying the work's totality and oneness. We may, for example, hear the performer suddenly adopt a too-distant and ill prepared new tempo or dynamic change for a given variation, exaggeration that seems to literally drop the listener onto a different musical planet. It can feel like the performer abruptly began a different piece of music. This is a great pity, because a close look at any good set of variations reveals many carefully graded steps taken by the original creator (the composer) to hold everything together as one single work. Artists will continue to be expressive through the louder spectrum of sound, recognizing that forte and fortissimo are not ends in themselves, but come with just as many different faces as do the dynamics of *piano* and *pianissimo.*

Please note in this performance how the seventeen variations are allowed to unfold organically, one by one from their original *chaconne* theme, each fully complementing the variation just played and leading thoughtfully into the next. In so doing the work is kept safe from the excesses that would threaten its structure and plunge it into seemingly unrelated parts.......

• • •

To cite again Torben Schousboe: "He [Nielsen] often advised his students to study counterpoint, not in order to become learned and complicated, but on the contrary to achieve greater strength and sincerity. These qualities are noticeable in his piano music." [EN 9-7] And biographer Robert Simpson contributes this observation: "[The *Chaconne*] achieves what Nielsen asserted to be impossible—a blend of a Bach-like contrapuntal feeling with a powerful dramatic impulse; the very elements, in fact, that brace Beethoven's last sonatas. Although this music sounds nothing like Beethoven's, it is astonishing to examine the texture and find that Beethoven is almost the only composer who anticipates some of its effects." [EN 9-8]

CHAPTER TEN

The Magyar Emigrant

Béla Viktor Jánâs Bartók, *Eight Improvisations on Hungarian Peasant Songs, op.20 (1920)*

Demaree

The sinking sun shone golden off the shields and lances of the sprawling mass of men; they rode brazenly, boldly, almost casually, over the eastern ridge and down a canyon into the broadening valley. Behind them a horde, looking disordered, but in fact clumped together into component "hundreds," stretched back for miles. Those shields and lances were not gold, but—at close range—rough wood, or even fabric. Few had metallic weaponry, yet almost all were well-protected by another feature of their horseback gear: pairs of stirrups! The guided missile of their day was the arrow, and their secret weapon was the stirrup. In battle they did not sit astride, but stood in those stirrups, and thus could pivot flexibly, so that they could fire *en masse* in something like a 300-degree arc, rather than generally straight ahead. Without taking time to turn the whole Magyar formation toward the enemy force, they could apply to their mounted forces—cavalry—the principle of *enfilade*. This military tactic apparently came from the Far East, and thus the Magyars had learned it from the larger nomadic tribes who were pushing them west. It proved devastating for a time, and so it terrified their Western opponents. **EN 10-1**

Béla Bartók signed photograph, 1922

Screened only by handfuls of scouts, who were pointing

Bartók at the piano

excitedly toward the west, rode a single figure with his right hand braced arrogantly on his hip, balancing the metallic shield on his left. Thus led the legendary Arpad, proud "king" of his nation of mounted warriors. Stretching back behind him and the small cluster of lesser chieftains who trailed him, their reputation already had caused monasteries as far west as Spain to pray to be spared "the arrows of the Hungarians." Although these tribesmen looked formidable, they actually were

Statue of Béla Bartók by Imre Varga, Siófok, Hungary

Legendary King Arpad of the Magyars (statue at Heroes' Square, Budapest, Hungary)

fleeing even-larger Oriental clans who had driven them out of their traditional grazing ranges.

These folk were the Magyars, viewing for the first time that very day the broad, richly fertile central valley expanding in front of them, below the Carpathian Mountains and beside the Danube: what would come to be known as the huge, fertile heart of Hungary, the "Carpathian Basin."

• • •

The haunting greatness of the Magyar past has enfolded the Hungarian present now for over twelve centuries. It is always there, linked to the ever-present current crises, to drive contemporary Hungarians to speak of and seek for heroism. They see themselves as the Spartans had at Thermopylae: they will lose against fearful odds, but their deaths will inspire. Leonidas's Greeks were not to fear death, nor the overwhelming storm cloud of Persian arrows; "Let them loose all they have, we will fight better in the shade!"

Over the centuries the Magyars sometimes won, and sometimes lost, but Hungary grew to dominate the Lower Danube basin and the Carpathians. The West broke the last Ottoman siege of Vienna in 1683 and then Prinz Eugen—later entombed in Vienna's *Stephansdom*—drove the Ottomans out of Central Europe for the last time. Prince Nicholaus I "the Magnificent" Esterhazy, employer of Joseph Haydn, was essentially Empress Maria Theresia's Hungarian viceroy, and he led in battle as her Captain her own hand-picked "Hungarian Bodyguard", who wore tiger skins over the shoulders of their splendid red-and-green uniforms. (For important social occasions this Prince wore his famous diamond-studded coat.)

In driving out the Ottomans, the Magyars found they had invited in the Habsburgs. The capital of Greater Hungary became Pressburg (now Slovakia's capital, Bratislava) and after World War I the diplomats made several new countries out of huge tracts of the Habsburg state—Czechoslovakia, Yugoslavia, Bulgaria, Romania, etc.[1]

Béla Bartók, born in that pre-war Greater Hungary, resented this geopolitical shrinkage all his life, and sought his Magyar fatherland back. Late in his "exile in the West" he reportedly said, "But I would like to go Home—forever." By "Home" he clearly meant "Greater" Hungary.

• • •

Intellectual brilliance, compositional imagination, pedagogical skills, performance **Artistry**: Béla Viktor Jánós Bartók was given it all. Yet, gauging by what he himself had to say about his life, in Europe and later in America, Bartók focused on complaining. He often felt mistreated and fostered the impression he and his wife were impoverished—had little of substance—that they were nothing short of living in hunger. Ostracized from his native Hungary by his own choice (for he feared and disapproved of the way his homeland was self-interestedly leaning toward Hitler's regime in the 1930s), Bartók and his second wife, Ditta Pásztory, spent much of the Second World War in an apartment in Forest Hills, New York. Thus, the composer could

---

1 Sir Winston Churchill wrote that "There is not one of the peoples or provinces that constituted the Empire of the Habsburgs to whom gaining their independence has not brought the tortures which ancient poets and theologians had reserved for the damned." EN 10-2

commute into the great city on business. EN 10-3 From there he and Ditta (who was also a fine—if somewhat limited—pianist) could set out on cross-country concert engagements.

Roughly contemporaneous with the war, Bartók's health became a legitimate factor in his complaining. Shoulder pain (obviously a serious issue for a pianist) is now thought by at least some to have been the first symptom of his final illness, leukemia. (His mid-1940s respites in the historic sanitorium site at Saranac Lake prompted many to assume that tuberculosis was the primal cause.)

Starving? In fact, that seems not to have been the case. Performance tours, teaching stipends, research grants, and gifts all flowed his way. An example: During his early days in America, he received a $3,000 grant from the Alice M. Ditson Fund to do work at Columbia University, with almost no stipulations as to his duties. (He himself chose to work on a huge ethnomusicological project.) In fact, in 1941-42, at the end of the Great Depression, $3,000 itself was the annual salary of a full professor at many ranking universities. Yet one of his biographers quotes out of a Bartók letter a typical expression of frustration:

> ...they [husband and wife] once spent three hours on the subway, "traveling hither and thither in the earth; finally, our time waning and our mission incomplete we shamefacedly slunk home—of course, entirely underground...") EN 10-4

In fact, just a few days earlier, Nobel Prize-winner Nicholas Murray Butler (no less) had conferred at Columbia University, where he was president, honorary doctorates on four internationally-recognized stars—in Bartók's case with the citation:

...distinguished teacher and master; ...creator through his composition of a musical style universally acknowledged to be one of the great contributions to the twentieth–century literature of music; a truly outstanding artist... [EN 10-5]

Thus, we must judge Bartók to have been a whiner! (So, for that matter, had been Mozart, Wagner, Schoenberg, and, perhaps worst of all, Beethoven—though the latter was rather more—a grouch!). Bartók's claims of "constant financial difficulties" he was apt to exaggerate all his life. [EN 10-6] The unhappy years that Bartók spent (so restive and resentful in America) resulted in his remarkable roster of culminative works—the evocative, imaginatively-formed *String Quartet No. 6*, for Yehudi Menuhin the *Sonata for Solo Violin*, the Ormandy-premiered (Piano) *Concerto No. 3*, William Primrose's *Viola Concerto* (the latter two works completed by Tibor Serly after the master's death), and above all Serge Koussevitsky's great commission, the 1943 *Concerto for Orchestra*. [EN 10-7]

Thus, we are offered at least one explanation of this complex man's attitudes: Bartók was a quintessential Magyar, especially proud of his homeland with its isolating Finno-Ugric tongue. He was bitterly resentful of the post-WW I treaties that had shredded his country into a small Balkan nation. He was bitterly resentful that many Hungarian immigrants were discarding their own command of their native language (a process that continued to be hurtful and divisive among the waves of fresh arrivals during the pre- and post-Hungarian Revolution years in the 1950s). He was bitterly resentful that the special Hungarian-language newspapers and radio stations were already beginning to die out in America, a land in which he thought himself forever an exile. He was—and would always have remained, one fears—utterly bitter and resentful. EN 10-8

Born in Nagyszentmiklós in 1881, by his twentieth birthday he had lived in at least seven villages, plus Budapest, Pressburg (the Hungarian capital at the time--now Bratislava), and Vienna itself. All save Vienna were in pre-war (that is World War I) "Greater Hungary." In the 1900s he saw himself primarily as a concert pianist and attacked the then-standard repertoire; in 1904-05 he made his first recordings of "Hungarian" folk music and began his perhaps-primary career as a musicologist. EN 10-9

It has not generally been noted that almost all the folk music he preserved in recording sessions was obtained from villages that were part of "Greater Hungary" before the Treaty of Versailles! He was still dedicated to preserving "Magyar culture" even from Hungarian villages that would become "Romanian", "Czech", "Slovak", or stand even behind the border of the USSR! These were not really "Hungarian" folk songs once Woodrow Wilson made them "Yugoslavian" or "Bosnian" or otherwise.

The piano maintained its centrality throughout his career. His lifelong dedication to the piano and its literature was as great as his near-lifelong dedication to ethnomusicology. EN 10-10 (He was, and remained, a splendid player. In his student years, especially in Budapest and Vienna, he apparently attempted to perform everything his countryman Liszt had written—and his performance of the *Totentanz* met with much enthusiasm.) He wrote one concerto for his and his wife's personal use, rather as financial security. His keyboard performances (both on church organ and piano) were the onset of his career, and his final composition (the last seventeen measures filled in by his student Tibor Serly) was *Piano Concerto No. 3*. His death in September 1945 denied him a living return to his motherland, and he was buried in Hartsfield, New York, an emigrant, but never an immigrant! **EN 10-11**

For recorded performance & commentary, please visit:
www.roberthamiltonpianist.com
Artistry: 8. Bartók, *Improvisations, op.20*

Eight Improvisations on Hungarian Peasant Songs

I.

CHAPTER TEN • 141

Recorded Voice-over remarks (printed version)

Hamilton

Last of all, let's look at the potentials before the **Artist** when a composer fully invites improvisation. I have in mind Béla Bartók's *Improvisations on Hungarian Peasant Songs, Opus 20.* While a lot of the improvisation is already provided by the composer, the perceptive pianist is inspired to launch a unique and personal creation, one that may differ significantly every time the work is performed. There are eight improvisations in the complete set. We will address three of them, beginning with the first. Here is interpretation number one of the first *Improvisation*....... If you are viewing the score, you note that this performance followed the markings very closely. The next version adopts a quicker 'Moderato' tempo, which makes more liberty possible....... And last, here is a version with more emphasis on the improvisational notes that Bartók added to the melody, as well as more contrast. This one demonstrates again that harmony provides color in music....... This first of eight *Improvisations* has what we might call three verses. The sixth *Improvisation i*n the set has four verses, each one of decreasing length. I will offer two versions of this *Improvisation*, the second of which explores much more and is longer: two minutes and ten seconds, to be exact, compared with the first version of just one minute and fifty seconds....... The seventh *Improvisation* on a Hungarian folk tune melody will provide the final example of this recording. It is dedicated to the memory of Claude Debussy, to whom Bartók's music owes a good deal. Among other devices, note the brief whole-tone insertion. And for one final time, please consider the wide variety of legitimate score interpretations that are possible! Although I present only two versions of this seventh *Improvisation*, the options are virtually unlimited, with differences both large and small.......

• • •

There was yet to be a final rounding of this composer's vivid overall life design. Bartók's wish to "return Home— forever" was actually fulfilled several years after his death in New York, when his body was re-interred near Budapest, next to Ditta. [EN] [10-12] The giant mounted figures near Arpad on the *Heldenplatz* no doubt cheered and reared their steeds to celebrate his arrival.

PART III
The Essence of Performing

"The artist tries and tries again to achieve the impossible.
Sometimes he is lucky and gets a little nearer to his goal...."
— Sergei Rachmaninoff ^{EN iii-1}

"...every performance is a different path up the mountain,
and nobody ever makes it all the way to the summit. That's
why we come back to the classics over and over again...."
— Terry Teachout ^{EN iii-2}

CHAPTER ELEVEN
Stage and Studio

Hamilton

Part I of this study identified a number of issues with **interpretation** and with verbal communication about music. Part II focused primarily on a group of composers, and on aural examples representing various ways of intuitively addressing works they composed.

We have sought to confront a simplistic, score-only approach to music performance that is widely accepted by students, teachers, scholars, critics, and some professional performers. In so doing we assert that no one can know precisely how past composers may have wished their created works to sound and to unfold—neither overall, nor in detail.

Some might find this heresy. As students we were/are taught that the *urtext* score *is* the work in each case, for it comes directly from the prime source and will never change so long as that *urtext* manuscript survives. And as noted in Chapter One, there are examples of some composers' struggles to get the music exactly "right"—in Beethoven's sketchbook modifications of the opening theme of the slow movement of the *Eroica*, for example, or his elaborate tempo superscriptions and (unreliable) metronome markings. Confronted with such data, it is tempting to believe that the manuscript exclusively provides all that is needed to perform a work with thorough comprehension.

But as we also note in Chapter One, beyond pitches and rhythms the printed score does not reveal much that is settled or complete. ^{EN 11-1} Therein lies the limitation of the printed *urtext* score. Most score markings from the composer must be acknowledged as mere points of departure, requiring thoughtful interpretation by the performer.

The Search for Meaning

How do we create interpretations that are not only personal, but licit as well?

A dedicated search for the message of a work is central. This search necessitates a lot of individual experimentation (supported by background studies of the composer and aural experiences with the composer's overall output). Much time needs to be spent freely trying things out with the music—certainly in advance of using practice repetition to secure an interpretation that is not yet developed! Such experimentation will also test limits. When the score requests a *ritardando*, for example, how much slowing (maximum amount) can be applied before we feel that the longer music line is being lost or stretched out of shape? Or conversely, what do we discover to be the minimum amount of slowing that avoids leaving the passage too straight or **rigid**? We cannot have a determination on such important matters until we try the passage in different ways to measure and resolve what sounds most balanced. These are judgment calls, and unless performers work at making such decisions, their performances will contain only what they have assumed (thoughtlessly) the composer wanted them to do. Such an approach is not only indefensible, it is a waste of the performer's instincts and originality.

Sergei Rachmaninoff the composer demanded much from himself as performer, including the revealing of what he termed "the point": "…he (Rachmaninoff) explained that each piece he plays is shaped around its culminating point; the whole mass of sounds must be so measured, the depth and power of each sound must be given with such purity and gradation that this peak point is achieved with an appearance of the greatest naturalness, though actually its accomplishment is the highest art. This moment must arrive with the sound and sparkle of a ribbon snapped at the end of a race—it must seem a liberation from the last material obstacle, the last barrier between truth and its expression. The composition itself determines this culmination; the point may come at its end or in the middle, it may be loud or soft, yet the musician must always be able to approach it with sure calculation, absolute exactitude, for if it slips by the whole structure crumbles, the work goes soft and fuzzy, and cannot convey to the listener what must be conveyed." [EN 11-2] His anxiety about this extended to others' performances of his music as well.

The "point" of which Rachmaninoff speaks is one of multitudes of questions that the score does not answer for us. In fact, the score can even confuse, as it does when this "point" happens to exist in one of several passages that are all indicated *fff* or *ffff*, for example. So, we must peer beyond the written manuscript to probe until we find answers.

As we probe and experiment, it is appropriate to question just how much one can freely create before a composition becomes essentially a reflection of the performer. To avoid this outcome, we must maintain focus on the original creator and creation. Otherwise, there is indeed the risk of creating a performer's own personal work which in the end may bear too little resemblance to the composer's message.

That said, many are alarmed to acknowledge the extent of interpretive freedom performing artists once employed. Although playfully scorned by colleagues as "The Puritan" for his "strict" adherence to the printed score, Rachmaninoff himself can be found in his own recordings to take astonishing liberties, at least by today's standards.

We suggest that with each new piece it is advantageous for the learner to initially proceed with free exploration, if not improvisation, wholly unrestrained by the score markings.[1] As important as these markings ultimately are, *they can subtly imprison our creative spirits*. There is plenty of opportunity to deal with the markings once a full personal response to the music has materialized. We must also be careful that a sense of duty to obey the composer does not cause us to add *more* forte, speed, etc. to what we have already felt, thus causing exaggerated effects. (Seasoned **Artists**, fully in touch with their own intuitions and

---

1   One might wish there were scores available which, like a Bach *urtext*, contain nothing but the notes. Such a clean source gives us complete freedom to first image the music from a personal perspective. The gifted would catch the overall design and purpose, making many fine interpretive decisions that are likely in line with the composer's own score markings (markings yet undiscovered). Then after **intuition** had led the way for a time, the fully marked score would be introduced and studied. Students would see where some details of their playing might not be in sync with the composer and work accordingly.

also accustomed to following their developed instincts, can adopt immediately a composer's markings without becoming enslaved in the process.)

As the saying goes, "beauty is in the eye (ear) of the beholder." Two people involved with the same work of art will usually find different things to emphasize, as well as differing ways of execution. This must be fully recognized and embraced. Most musicians have had interactions with their peers that reveal sharp differences of perception. Occasionally discussion at examinations or competitions will grow impassioned and intense. Such communication demonstrates deep concern and is healthy for music, an art that thrives in part because of its variety of valid interpretations. How tiresome it would be if everyone revealed a nocturne in the same way. Because we are individuals, our discoveries will be different. And can anyone ever be certain of finding the *definitive* essence of a work?

One encounters live and recorded performances by professionals and non-professionals which are really only shallow copies of compelling interpretations by Artists. How long will consumers keep wanting to hear performances in which they are given only the outer shells of composers' creations. It is not enough that performers produce the correct notes, stay in tempo and apply fine contrasts—if there is little originality or awareness of a message. Perhaps we find a parallel in the many paintings for sale, often from skilled artists, which are their own painted copies of masterworks from great painters of the past. The impacts of purpose and originality are somehow missing. (Is it possible that too many imitative performances have something to do with dwindling music audiences in some parts of the world?)

On the micro level it is important that a performance gives

relevant meaning to every individual note that is played, which can in turn build meaningful motives and ultimately reveal a message. Whether on the piano or some other instrument, it is unfortunately possible to produce notes that are devoid of content. A performer might be distracted by wandering thoughts, by proper posture or the positioning of fingers, or by an excessive desire for technical display; even the effort to create colorful tone qualities can get in the way of a note's meaning and purpose. Such distractions may involve important things, but the absence of perceived meaning within a note of music is just as damaging as it would be for a spoken word. Envision a non-English-speaking person pronouncing an unfamiliar word like "won-der-ful", employing fine mechanical care and skill, but completely unaware of what it means. Will we immediately (and fully) understand it? Possibly not. And the situation becomes worse as more words (or notes) coalesce in an effort to form the intended ideas and purpose.

Some Thoughts

We must bear in mind that all languages, music included, are means through which ideas are expressed. Music ideas are not purely intellectual or emotional, but both. Our duty as performers is to discover, put together and express ideas with as much clarity, intelligence and emotional honesty as we can muster—in each and every performance that we give.

Sound is, of course, our basic raw material in music. In past eras pianists and other musicians liked to develop a signature sound, and it was often possible to identify them by their sound alone. They took a great deal of pride in the unique tone qualities they could create. Creating special sounds is now often bypassed in the pursuit of other endeavors. This neglect side-steps the variety of tonal colors which the modern piano is capable of producing. Imaginative use of the pedals to create color is also overlooked. Rachmaninoff and others reportedly considered the damper (sustaining) pedal to be the very "soul" of the piano. But pedals can be relegated to nothing more than simple aids for playing softer or sustaining notes and chords—a sad waste of a valuable resource. (Composers have possibly wished, on occasion, for the unique effects of the piano's pedals when creating their music for orchestra or other ensembles.)

Some might question the piano's ability to provide color. After all, the piano basically produces one timbral sound, not at all like the orchestra with its wide variety of stringed, wind and percussive sounds. But timbral color is only surface color. The deeper color of music resides in its harmony (including melodic tones) and in nuanced harmonic changes, regardless of medium or instruments. It can take time to hear and fully appreciate this, perhaps with engaged slower listening for the sole purpose of experiencing the substantial difference between, say, a C-sharp major chord and one in E major. Once we become sensitive to this, we can open an exciting new world in performance. We are not, of course, speaking of visual colors (except for people with synesthesia who perceive both visual and aural colors simultaneously). But comparisons can be made with the visual world: black-and-white versus color films, for instance.[2]

---

2   Films in color will generally dampen and disguise the deeper factors of contrast, shading and nuance, elements that are especially notable and effective in black and white films. Clever cinematography can sometimes shape and limit color usage to minimize this problem.

There is a need for attention to melody—or that which could be considered the main line of music communication. Fine conductors and chamber musicians can readily promote good projection and shaping of melodic lines. Solo pianists, however, must independently produce both melody and accompaniment on one instrument, and it's likely that melodic organization and projection are frequently minimized or neglected during preparation.[3] This can happen because a single melody line is usually easy to play at sight on the piano, whereas the accompaniment contains many more notes of far greater combined difficulty. The accompaniment therefore consumes more of the pianist's time and attention. Some pianists may not realize when a point is reached where the accompaniment has unintentionally become primary, with many of the melody notes frankly just filling in as the music moves along. This means that the essential melody line is failing to take its leadership role. A good ritual for pianists is to rehearse segments of the melody alone each day, not only to improve its shape and tone, but also to help maintain the ear's chief focus where it needs to be. If one considers a song or an instrumental piece with piano accompaniment, the soloist spends many hours of practice on just the melody line. Thus, the final performance presents a carefully prepared melody, as well as prepared accompaniment. With solo piano music, pianists cannot do complete justice to the melodic meaning, color, organization, and articulation if the melody is *only* practiced in

---

3 The author recalls one of his doctoral students playing a Chopin nocturne just a week before her final degree recital. She had played it beautifully many times, but on this occasion, something was noticeably off. He asked her to play a portion of the melody, alone, with no accompaniment. After doing so a couple of times, she was instructed to add back the accompaniment. Immediately all was in order again, similar to hitting a reset button.

combination with the many accompaniment notes that demand attention. For critical melodic lines to be fully prepared, they need to receive separate focus.

It is evident that many young performers spend so much time trying to achieve equal definition for every single note that, to varying degrees, they ignore the fundamental principle of "grouping." Grouping pertains to the ordering and shaping of individual notes with proper inflection and pulse, rather than playing all notes at the same volume. It implies accent points that are surrounded with lighter tones. To produce all notes at equal strength leads to shapeless music (like a bad lecturer speaking in a monotone). Many students do not realize this is happening, because their attentions are directed excessively to technical accomplishment. Such practice can also lead to physical tightness and injuries.

Pacing is a fascinating topic. Many of us need to sense more effectively, within ourselves, the natural points of rest in the music we perform. A temptation is to keep barreling forward, leaving the music breathless. Performers must remember that music was first sung, and singers have to *breathe*. One can learn from the two ancient Greek concepts of time: *Chronos* and *Kairos. Chronos* is regular clock and calendar time, whereas *Kairos* measures time by special opportune or destined moments. Students readily adopt the former, represented in music by the metronome or teacher insisting on a steadier beat. But *Kairos* involves the equally important factor of sensing the moment when something *should* occur, or when the music needs to rest, and then stepping outside of regulated time enough to allow for the arrival or unfolding. At such moments, *Kairos* must be given the power to overrule *Chronos* time, to achieve the fullest possible expression of an important happening. Yet another helpful principle comes from the Dalcroze Eurythmics Method, which is the relating of body movements to the rhythms of music. One such correlation is between the distance of footsteps and skips in music. Because we need more time to take large footsteps, our music performing becomes more intuitive and rewarding when we do the same with large tonal skips. Unfortunately, some performers work excessively on these difficult large skips until they can jump back and forth in perfect metronomic time. The pity is that this extended practice effort is counterproductive due to the less satisfying musical result. Humans intuitively relate to the Eurythmic principle and enjoy being permitted to experience the natural ebb and flow of music. Some need to remember that we are not preparing to perform for an audience of mechanical metronomes.

Another important concept that has been referred to earlier is to avoid playing a piece each time in exactly the same way. Following this practice can inhibit our growth in perception and understanding, as well as cause loss of freshness and originality. Likewise, we should generally not repeat a given passage of a piece in the same way. This is relevant because music exists in time, yearning to move forward to an ultimate destination. When we perform a passage again in altogether the same manner, it can make listeners feel as if they have been abandoned in one spot, or even dropped back towards the beginning again. There are many reports of composers' own diversity in playing, such as the aforementioned extraordinary experience of Julius Seligmann at a Chopin concert. ^{EN 11-3}

Regarding dynamics, many musicians unfortunately perform *forte* and *fortissimo* in much the same way every single time, irrespective of the piece or of its specific character at any given moment. When creating soft to middle dynamic ranges, they may exhibit refined judgments. But when the music asks for more force, they seem content with merely "loud" (or even worse with all of the notes at equal volume, a state which the author's teacher, Sidney Foster, called "unrelieved *forte*"). We need to remind ourselves that character should never be abandoned, and that there are many varieties of loud sound—triumphant, majestic, stormy, etc.—each presented with a certain roundness or sharpness of attack. One hears performances where the loud moments have little shape or purpose, while the quieter passages are given the greatest of care (sometimes to the point of exaggerated self-expression, as if to make up for the previous noise).

On Stage

In performance, the beginning can be determinative. Among other things, it is important to intuit the optimal tempo—a relative and individual matter. While it needs to be in accordance with the composer's direction, the actual speed which best satisfies the charge at any given time will differ between individuals, as well as between a performer's own performances. The "optimal" tempo is that which most successfully matches the essence of a work with the existing performance conditions. It is not immutable but correlates with the performer's current physical/mental/ spiritual disposition, as well as with the instrument at hand, the acoustics of the room, and the nature of the audience. As the performer's mental command and physical skills improve during preparations, a tempo which once sounded fast may now convey moderation, or slowness, if held back when the mind and body are feeling the music at a faster speed. However, it is always crucial that the tempo not exceed the performer's ability to comfortably rise above all technical challenges, so as to permit full execution of the meaning and emotion of the music (*e.g.*, joy).

Once found, the tempo must have consistency if the various motives and rhythms of a piece are to be revealed in their proper relationships.[4] At the same time, tempo **rigidity** in performance is undesirable. There are moments when music clearly wants to lean forward, or hold back slightly, and these small adjustments can be done without altering the established speed or pulse. Czerny once made these perceptive remarks: "Before everything else, we must consider it as a rule, always to play each piece of music, from beginning to end, without the least deviation or uncertainty, in the time prescribed by the Author, and first fixed upon by the Player. But without injury to this maxim, *there occurs almost in every line some notes or passages, where a small and often almost imperceptible relaxation or acceleration of the movement is necessary, to embellish the expression and increase the interest.*" [EN 11-4] (emphasis added)

Serious Artists with something important to "say" will come across to audiences as compelling. To be compelling requires intensity. This is an elusive factor (difficult to teach or to pass on to another) in attracting and maintaining attention. Intensity is important in both loud and soft passages, perhaps even more so in the latter. In the words of American composer-pianist Ernst

---

4 Sometimes performers will set a good pulse, only to lose it as the piece progresses. When the pulse is weakened in quicker movements, speeds will often move ahead so much that the music seems to be running away from itself. This can happen due to insufficient control of our emotions in a performance.

Bacon: "If there is one trait common to all great interpreters, it is their *capacity for intensification*. There are many ways to achieve intensity, dictated by the music; but whether explosive, impassioned, eloquent or restrained, intensity will always be felt as a mark of inner energy. Without this intensity, the listener never more than half listens. But when it is there, his attention is drawn in ratio to the player's concentration; he feels what the player communicates, on whatever level it may be." **EN 11-5**

As the need arises, performers aspire to create brilliance on-stage with their speed and loudness. A sometimes-unconscious misconception is that brilliance increases simply with the escalation of speed. In actuality, the faster a passage is played the lighter it must be, to enable the performer to move more quickly. And as it grows lighter it becomes less brilliant. We have limits to our physical energy, and playing at our maximum speed and maximum volume simultaneously is not attainable. Brilliance comes, then, from achieving an effective *balance* of speed and volume in any given passage. "Brilliance", Bacon suggests, "is neither speed nor loudness alone. Speed beyond a certain point defeats itself. Successive sounds, when very fast, begin to be grouped in the mind and lose their character of individual pulsation. A well-articulated, fairly rapid passage may give more impression of swiftness than a faster passage played beyond all perception of its swift detail. Likewise, a large sound, pushed beyond its limits of sonority, will become harsh and defeat itself in acoustical corrugation." **EN 11-6**

There is damage that can be done to music by *rubato* that is excessive or overly rehearsed. Sometimes it is better to use nuance and articulation to express an idea fully, as *rubato* can interrupt flow and momentum. Often while on tour, there is a sort of "rubato-creep" as one performs the same piece over and over again. The author remembers such an experience with Chopin's *B-Minor Sonata*. He had just performed it many times on a European tour, arriving home a couple of weeks before a Town Hall concert in New York City. While practicing at home, it seemed that the work had somehow lost its essence and overall meaning. So, he began playing it through with all rubato removed. As everything straightened out, the sonata's natural beauty returned. (He has since found that to play through learned works, perhaps once every three times without *rubato*, avoids excessive buildup and encourages the use of more sophisticated nuances.)

It is understandable that a performer's unfolding life with a piece might see gradual drifting into more and more *rubato* as it is played repeatedly. In each performance we try to fully express the piece to our audience, and last night's rubato effects may feel insufficient for tonight's performance. Eventually, the delicate balance between tempo regularity and *rubato* can become distorted. As pianist, Sergei Rachmaninoff certainly understood this problem, and reportedly took regular steps to avoid the trap of performance excess and sloppiness.[5]

---

5 According to author-pianist Abram Chasins: "Rachmaninoff was a dedicated and driven perfectionist. He worked incessantly, with infinite patience. Once I had an appointment to spend an afternoon with him in Hollywood. Arriving at the designated hour of twelve, I heard an occasional piano sound as I approached the cottage. I stood outside the door, unable to believe my ears. Rachmaninoff was practicing Chopin's etude in thirds, but at such a snail's pace that it took me a while to recognize it because so much time elapsed between each finger stroke and the next. Fascinated, I clocked this remarkable exhibition; twenty seconds per bar was his pace for almost an hour while I waited riveted to the spot, quite unable to ring the bell. Perhaps this way of developing and maintaining an unerring mechanism accounted for his bitter sarcasm toward colleagues who practiced their programs 'once over lightly' between concerts." EN 11-7

Stage fright is a topic that is sometimes best left undiscussed, such as in the company of those who may be free of its destructive influence. Teachers are arguably better off working separately with affected students. Stage fright emerges from the common pre-concert nervousness that virtually everyone experiences. Those who cannot control their nerves, however, may find themselves succumbing to fear, which has the potential to ruin hundreds of hours of diligent preparation. Legendary pianist Vladimir Horowitz had the problem to deal with, reportedly needing to be literally pushed onto the stage at times. But he knew how to channel his fears into an excitement which was felt by all of us who heard him. Ernst Bacon has a helpful suggestion for easing the problem in advance: "Since fear can sometimes paralyze play in public, one must not only 'shore up' every weak point in a work's preparation (the anticipation of or stumbling through which, is perhaps the chief reason for fear), but one should *deliberately practice non- fear, forbid the intrusion of anxiety. Self-assurance can be practiced.*" EN 11-8 (emphasis added.) This practice of "non-fear" or confidence ought to be applied during our purely mental rehearsing as well. With consistent effort, new habits can be formed, and anxiety diminished. Many do not face their gathering fears early enough as a concert draws near, permitting fear to be their unwelcome partner during performance.

One revered accomplishment in performing is to convey the impression that a work is being made up or created on the spot, unique, and in the immediate presence of the audience. Another term would be improvising. It involves the willingness to take risks. A general plan is already in place, of course, but to venture outside the usual boundaries here and there is the objective, opening the way to some special moments. And such moments are what listeners will likely retain long after the concert is over, because the moments were special and offered just for them. The alternative of sticking unbendingly to all details of the plan, sometimes even forcing ourselves (or an uncooperative instrument) to comply, creates the effect of merely reciting what has been done repeatedly in the practice room. It can be boring.

Composers and Performing

In the course of this book, we have offered selected data that indicate the great composer-pianists did not hesitate to be free with their own printed scores or add new ideas as they performed. And as posited in the recorded voiceover remarks on Chopin: why should we think it best to play a composer's work with limited and strict adherence to the score, when even the composer did not do so?

Composers compose or create their works in a general state of freedom. But what of the creations of performers? Perhaps we should repeatedly remind ourselves that Music, from the beginning, has emerged from virtually free creative exploration and expression—and not from the fixed, lifeless printed pages before us. Sadly, the very printed symbols in the score have the potential to seize our sole devotion, dampening our independent spirits. If composers create in freedom, *so must performers.*

It would be wonderful to know more about how pre-recording-era composers performed their own music. Acquiring a full understanding is unlikely, however. As leading Bach/Baroque scholar Anthony Newman writes: "Because (J. S.) Bach wrote nothing about the performance of his own works, we have to consult his contemporaries, friends, family and students. We will never be able to know exactly how Bach played his own music…. it is quite impossible to know exactly how a composer wants something to sound unless he is present in the flesh to tell us. But even if Bach himself were alive to demonstrate, any given piece would not be performed the same way twice; I believe this is especially true given the 18th-century aesthetic and its high proclivity towards improvisation." EN 11-9

We are frequently reminded that improvising was common among performers of the Baroque and Classic periods, and perhaps on into the early twentieth century as well (at which point some of it shifted to jazz). Such musicians were not "pure" performers as so many of us are today, but participants in the composing process as well. Because improvising eliminates the printed page, the practice can train us to maintain focus on the music itself (rather than the score) while we learn and play. As musicians have tended away from the practice of improvisation, a tyranny of the score has taken its place. When there is loss of creative curiosity and only acceptance of dead notes marked on a page, performers are then, frankly, engaging in a paint-by-the-numbers activity.

Since it is given that we will never know for certain how a composer like Bach performed his own music, we must acknowledge that the score cannot so inform us either. We are largely on our own. And to those who might be tempted to approach the music of Bach with a rigid, one-way adherence to the score, Mr. Newman offers this: "There are often several possible solutions. The only impossible solution is that the music…be played with metronomic regularity. A false tradition dies slowly, however.

Perhaps a single work of Bach's might be looked at to convince the skeptical performer of the necessity of time freedom in general: the *Allemande* to the solo flute *Partita in A Minor, S. 1013,* sixty-five measures of uninterrupted sixteenth notes. Where do you breathe? The conclusion is unavoidable!" EN 11-10

J.S. Bach's son, C.P.E. Bach, wrote the "Essay on the True Art of Playing Keyboard Instruments" which Harold C. Schonberg duly observes "influenced the playing of the entire classic period. He (Bach) even has a lengthy paragraph on the tempo *rubato*, which may come as a surprise to those who consider *rubato* a romantic phenomenon. Bach was one of the first to describe it (although, of course, it was always used; music without *rubato* would be so inhumanly metronomic as to be unlistenable)."EN 11-11 *Rubato* is sometimes shunned by performers who, mistakenly, believe the music of Haydn and Mozart should be played in strict tempo and rhythm.

Schonberg goes on to say this about the freedom of Mozart's performances: "The chances are that Mozart never played any of his compositions twice the same way. In 1783 he wrote home that whenever he played his *D Major Concerto (K. 175),* 'I always play what occurs to me at the moment'." EN 11-12

The playing of Beethoven was disclosed by some of his students. One such student was the Baroness Ertmann who studied with Beethoven for many years. "Schindler described her sense for 'free tempo' as instructive, adding that no one had reproduced Beethoven's own manner of playing as closely as she". EN 11-13And from a letter Mendelssohn wrote to his sister: "She (Baroness Ertmann) plays the Beethoven things beautifully...often exaggerates the expression a little and holds back a great deal and then hurries again..."EN 11-14 Also: "Schindler (says) that all the pieces he himself heard Beethoven play were, with hardly any exceptions, thoroughly free and flexible". [EN 11-15]

F.G. Wegeler (physician and childhood friend of Beethoven) & Ferdinand Ries (Beethoven's former pupil and close associate) wrote in their 1838 Beethoven biography: "In general he played his compositions very whimsically; nevertheless, he usually kept a steady beat and only occasionally pushed the tempo..."[EN 11-16] Schonberg cautions that Ries's statement about Beethoven keeping a steady beat must be taken relatively. For Beethoven's time, his metrical pulse was indeed considered steady. But by our current standards, it would likely have varied far too much (Schonberg uses the word "intolerable"). "We would consider his performances sheer anarchism if he returned today, while he would listen to current Beethoven specialists and consider them dry, unmusical and anything but expressive." [EN 11-17]

Two contributions from the master himself are instructive. Following the performance of one of his sonatas by Marie Bigot de Moroques, Beethoven was said to have commented: "That is not exactly the reading I should have given, but go on. If it is not exactly myself, it is something better." [EN 11-18] And Adolf Bernhard Marx revealed what Beethoven had written about tempo in one of his songs: "On the autograph of the song 'Nord oder Sud' one can clearly read, in Beethoven's hand: '100 according to Maelzel, but this is only valid for the first measures, since feeling also has its beat, which however cannot be expressed completely by this tempo (namely, 100)." [EN 11-19]

Ignaz Moscheles, another of Beethoven's pupils, came out with his own edition of the sonatas following Beethoven's death. He said he was guided by memories of the master's playing, and "...I hope in this new publication to be permitted to complete, with traditional correctness, many a gap in the signs of interpretation which Beethoven played but did not write down…and which every intelligent musician can add…" EN 11-20

Czerny is perhaps the best known of Beethoven's pupils, and among the strictest. But "strict" had different implications in those times: "If so strict a pedagogue as Czerny allowed a liberal use of *ritards* and interpolations, one can imagine what the romantics did. Czerny, in his *Klavierschule*, allows *ritards* practically everywhere—at the return of the principal subject; when a phrase is to be separated from the melody; on strongly accented long notes; at a transition to a different tempo; after a pause; at the *diminuendo* of a quick passage; in a *crescendo* passage; at the introduction or end of an important passage; in passages 'where the composer or performer gives free rein to his fancy' (which could mean anywhere); when the composer writes expressive; at the end of a trill or cadence." EN 11-21

Regarding the wide abandon of the Romantic era, we read this from Schonberg: "Throughout the nineteenth century… very few instrumentalists played the notes exactly as written. Nor did singers bother much with the printed note." EN   Also: "There was hardly a musician in the nineteenth century, and that includes such intellectual stalwarts as Clara and Robert Schumann…who did not see in any specific piece of music a message far outstripping the written note." EN 11-22

Noted Anglo-German pianist and conductor, Sir Charles Halle, heard Chopin perform on multiple occasions, and wrote these comments: "A remarkable feature of his playing was the entire freedom with which he treated the rhythm." And: "He played the latter part of his *Barcarolle*, when it demands the utmost energy, in the most opposite style, *pianissimo*, but with such wonderful nuances." EN 11-23 Even allowing for reports about Chopin's poor physical condition at the time, such a dramatic reversal is testimony to his willingness to take great performance liberties.

The freedom of Liszt in performance is legendary and widely acknowledged. One eye-witness report affirms that even correctness of the printed note was, for him, secondary to the overall effect of his music. The American concert pianist, Amy Fay (who studied with the master), wrote this after a Liszt concert she witnessed: "He was rolling up the piano in *arpeggios* in a very grand manner indeed, when he struck a semi-tone short of the high note [with] which he had intended to end. I caught my breath and wondered whether he was going to leave us like that, in mid-air, as it were, the harmony unresolved, or whether he would be reduced to the humiliation of correcting himself like ordinary mortals, and taking the right chord. A half smile came over his face, as much as to say—'Don't fancy that this little thing disturbs me'—and he instantly went meandering down the piano in harmony with the false note he had struck, and then rolled deliberately up in a second grand sweep, *this* time striking true. I never saw a more delicious piece of cleverness. It was so quick-witted and so exactly characteristic of Liszt. Instead of giving you a chance to say, 'He has made a mistake,' he forced you to say, 'He has shown how to get out of a mistake'." EN 11-24

Perhaps the playing of Mendelssohn stayed more within the boundaries of the printed score than the majority of his contemporaries. But nonetheless, writes Schonberg, his playing "must have been free, spirited." Consider Mendelssohn's own words regarding certain sections of J.S. Bach's Chromatic

Fantasy and Fugue: "I take the liberty of playing them with all possible *crescendos*, and *pianos*, and *fortissimos*, pedal of course, and to double the octaves in the bass." [EN 11-25] And Schonberg recalls that "it was Mendelssohn who, in his famous 1829 revival of Bach's St. Matthew Passion, did not hesitate to chop, cut, alter and modernize it." [EN 11-26]

Following the Romantics, piano performance tradition carried on in the free Romantic spirit for a while. But by the middle of the twentieth century there was increased emphasis on mechanical perfection and a stricter reading of scores. Undoubtedly one influence for change was the dawn of the second industrial revolution at the turn of the century, bringing its machinery of perfection and primitive rhythms. The output of major composers was clearly influenced, as shown in early twentieth century works like *Allegro Barbaro (Sz.49)* by Béla Bartók (1911), *Toccata, Opus 11* by Sergei Prokofiev (1912), and *The Rite of Spring* (1913) by Igor Stravinsky. And now, with our modern world of computers, cell phones and gadgets carrying us even farther from the simplicity of Nature, it's no surprise that our music and performing are reacting in kind. "When listening to pianists born before 1875, or trying to visualize how they played", states Schonberg, "it is necessary for us in the latter half of the twentieth century to change our entire concept about the very nature of music." [EN 11-27]

Of course, we can enjoy recordings of some of these pianists who were born before 1875, beginning with one of the most important, Sergei Rachmaninoff. It is not only entertaining, but instructive to compare their playing with the printed scores, especially when it is a Rachmaninoff performing his own music in a deviating way. Or Artur Schnabel performing a Beethoven *Sonata* differently from the way he edited it in his very own edition.

A Brief Word on Teaching

If the desire is to cultivate **Artistry**, it seems logical that teachers will work as much as possible at all levels to discover, encourage and shape the individual perceptions *of their students*. Thoughtful instruction will reveal some of the variety of acceptable interpretive possibilities. In the process, boundaries of taste and culture may be addressed so that each student accrues important knowledge for future endeavors. There will be additional opportunities for students to gather differing perspectives, including participation in master classes, summer festivals and competitions.

An interesting issue concerns the upsides and downsides of demonstrating by the teacher. In a way, it seems preferable for the teacher to demonstrate as little as possible during lessons, because when a teacher plays to illustrate something, the student picks up more than just the matter at hand. With too-frequent demonstrating, students could soon be revolving their interpretations around what the teacher does, instead of employing their own personal intuitive responses. This can happen whether the teacher intends it or not, and it would seem best to avoid regularly distracting students from their own paths of discovery.

That said, it sometimes proves necessary to actually demonstrate good sound and direction for a student. Or there may be so many things to correct that a demonstration is the most practical approach. Especially in more basic teaching, demonstrating can move things along more quickly ("a picture is worth a thousand words"). It is further true that even many of the great composers began by imitating other composers, and for children we have developed highly imitative approaches for the young (e.g. Suzuki Method) that have proved successful.

Still, those composers and performers who imitated for very long are largely unknown or forgotten, while the greats were given (or seized) the opportunity to find their own original ways of communicating through music. If a student is to develop individual Artistry, an independent and personal search for meaning must be encouraged. Copying a teacher's playing—or imitating an admired recording—tends to move students away from this goal.[6]

Perhaps, then, the use of imitation should be reserved for those lessons in which verbal instructions are insufficient. An effective and less intrusive practice is for the teacher to lightly play given notes as the student is playing to gently guide such matters as shaping, voicing, achieving tonal beauty and maintaining a steady pulse. This is less likely to promote direct copying.

There are times when piano teachers are obliged to teach with only one piano in the room, which forces them to rely more on word pictures. Singing along while students play is also potentially helpful.

While direct imitation can be the easiest way of helping a student sound better, care should be taken that it does not inhibit the student's important pursuit of a personal Artistry.

---

6 With the easy accessibility of recordings on the internet, some students may be copying other pianists more than they are adopting the teacher's instructions.

CHAPTER TWELVE

Taste and Trust

Demaree & Hamilton

But who shall judge the judges...?

In chapters Three through Ten the present authors examined nine prominent composers, seeking to provide background data and evidence—with the aid of voice-over recordings and **Spiral Study** reviews—that the mere score is not sufficient for a composer to reveal exactly how the performer should reproduce a work; in short, that even the *urtext* (let alone one of the often carelessly idiosyncratic editions) is an incomplete blueprint for the **interpretation** of a given work of music. We have found explicit evidence that the composers themselves often interpreted their notated creations in ways different from their written directions.

Yet famed performers frequently swear exclusive allegiance to "the score"—this though their own performances, like the composers', may belie such loyal dedication. Experience suggests that it is rare to encounter a professional performance which adheres to all of the score's written details. The question is how such license should be granted, to whom, and where the boundaries should lie.

If we can agree that the **Artist** has the experience and judgment to imbue aspects of the engraved score with the sort of freedom offered by author/pianist Hamilton in the provided recordings, what are the outer limits we should expect him and his peers to accept? Are performances to be (1) carefully pre-planned, **rigid** repetitions of each other, or at the opposite extreme, (2) promiscuous free-for-alls that are always different, but devoid of a good plan? Must we settle for the sketchily-known preferences of composers (often deceased), or performers mainly seeking personal attention, or audience members who lack serious interest and perspective? And who shall decide? Who shall speak for Ives? Who shall judge—referee—indeed?

One widely-accepted answer is that the music of various periods must be rendered with "good **taste**." To describe a concert performance as "**tasteful**" is to turn to the five senses to approximate the effect of a certain approach to that work as if it were delectable, rather than foul in flavor (like adding the wrong spices to a specific food dish). In another era—another culture—certain choices may be traditionally engrained, and thus please those individuals' senses.

But how does one acquire this communal bias toward tastefulness in food and, for our purposes here, in Music? The reader has been offered what was described as the Spiral Study. [EN 12-1] The sincere Artist does not simply "practice" playing the work, but experiments and studies all of its brethren, geographical settings, forerunners, and successors.

The Clouded Brain

For centuries, all sorts of folk have acknowledged that music, like the visual arts, ballet, and certain other genres, is a distinct language (a word generally assumed to refer to verbal communication). And centuries have also been devoted to attempts to translate these other "systems of expression" into the various verbal tongues. Great thinkers have sought to directly equate organized music with the "sentences" or "structures" of verbal languages. But aside from certain shared performance aspects (e.g., pausing briefly after a given idea or thought), none of these attempts fully convinces the present authors, who have found direct "translations" from music to English, or German, or Russian verbiage limiting. We are persuaded that Music is an independent, untranslatable language system, capable of conveying its own sensitive and potent meanings to those who have heard and studied it.

Now begins a new era: at this point, current brain research at major universities is pertinent to the readers' understanding of these concepts. The slang-like term "cloud" in the present day is commonplace and can refer informally to an encyclopedic storehouse of words and related concepts. As one grows and learns, inescapable connections (relationships) are apparently stored in an individual's brain (technically, in the meninges, the outer layer[s] covering the brain) to be triggered whenever a related reference is experienced. For example, an American hearing the words "Four score and seven years ago..." is likely to immediately call to mind the words "Lincoln" and "Gettysburg" from personal verbal experience—that is, one's English language "cloud." EN 12-2 This recollection is thought to be unsought and unavoidable, though a typical Laplander would be unlikely to experience it. Researchers at UC Berkeley and the University of Houston are among those engaged in this current and ongoing cognitive research. EN 12-3 Thus far, their focus has been primarily on the "word cloud," that is to say, verbal correspondences, and the like. However: "…scientists are trying to find how our brains mix sensory impressions of color, texture, and shape with memory, meaning, and emotion into aesthetic judgment of artworks…" EN 12-4

Think again of our Spiral Study. Can it be doubted that the realms of music are, or will be, among the next "languages" for these scientists to approach? Are our "style studies" both necessary and inevitable? Are our best, most **Artistic** performance choices brain-driven, not merely ephemeral, impromptu, and transient?

And what does this imply about searches for "good taste" in Music. Does it not suggest that such parallel Spiral Studies develop in Artists separate realms of fitting—but differing— interpretations for Mozart vs. Sebastian Bach vs. Beethoven vs. Machaut? Is this the rationale for using a different style and magnitude of *rubato* in Baroque performance than the Romantic? Does an unrecognized "Mozart-piano-sonata-cloud" impose limitations not relevant to Chopin or Bartók? (A Spiral Study of a Beethoven piano sonata applies such limits of style to Beethoven's score, not to the works of Chopin— or of John Cage!)

Assume a virtue, if you have it not… EN 12-5

Regarding trust, let us first agree that music does not belong primarily to either composers, performers, or consumers. Each of these groups has its prejudices. Music comes, and is intended for all, as a wondrous gift. Trust must be earned, not just by one faction, but by all. The composer must take the various elements available and construct sincere and honorable works which represent his or her best possible efforts; the performer must approach each composition with full respect and openness, striving through arduous study and discipline to earn the trust of both composer and listener; and finally the latter must give full attention, both emotional and intellectual, to each performed work. This three-way bond of trust must be shared if music is to survive and exist at its highest levels.

"Assume a virtue," Hamlet advises his mother, the once and once-again Queen, thus urging that she deny herself to his uncle, the villainous new King. Will she be able to trust herself? Will the Artist be willing and able to exhaustively and sufficiently study the milieu spiraling around a work that he or she intends to perform? In all human endeavors, virtue may be earned, as well as rewarded. Repeated study enables one to trust oneself, and gradually encircles the novice with a routine that constitutes a lifelong commitment to such study.

Whatever limits we establish as **Artistic**, we come gradually to surround our performances with our personal **stylistic** identity. Much of this can become standard but must never become routine. In general, there are outer boundaries in music which most of us will accept, boundaries that seem imprinted upon the music itself, regardless of the stylistic period. For example, a delicate little piece with simple texture and line from any period or composer will rebel against a performer's use of exaggerated dynamics or *rubato*. And it makes no difference whether it's from the early classical period or a simple, fragile work of Prokofiev.

Who shall choose between alternative "outer boundaries"?

This question emerges in the search for taste, and also in matters such as our treatment of works of differing length. Performing larger structures is significantly different from performing short pieces (or movements). To some extent short pieces can be well executed on the piano simply with refined touch sensitivity and an emotional identification with the work, while longer *opera* will demand a more studied and extensive intellectual wisdom.

Success with larger forms requires performers to see and think on a grand scale. Those who are persuasive with shorter forms may present renditions of variation works (e.g. Beethoven, Brahms) that reflect insufficient awareness of how the variations fit together to create one single, unfolding structure. [EN 12-6] Changes of *tempi* and dynamics may be added, or greatly exaggerated to make an individual variation sound as impressively contrasting as possible, while unfortunately losing its relationship with surrounding variations. The predictable result is structural confusion. In such performances, listeners will not easily experience the collective work as a whole—with continual movement to its destination—but rather as an array of unconnected moments. Other large forms have suffered similar performance fates, as the outer boundaries of good taste are ignored.

Then there are the endless references to "inspirational" and "emotional" foundations for a performance. This often seems an excuse for unjustifiable interpretations: an attempt to explain radical departures from the clear spirit of the original work. And how critical such departures can prove to be! But at the opposite extreme, the loss of a work's meaning during extensive preparations (or from too-frequent performing) can cause some public performances to become uninspired readings or walk-throughs.

Composers and audiences are at the mercy of performers and must trust them to bring forth the music's visions. But with the common assumption that score details are absolute and unbending, it can be difficult to accept **intuition** as playing a role. How might the use of intuition affect the composer's confidence in an Artist to honor the former's notated intentions? And as asked previously, "How does a workmanlike musician become an Artist? What should be the principal goals?" EN 12-7

The reader will recall another passage in the introduction to Part II, EN 12-8 in which we quoted German baritone Matthias Goerne arguing the primacy of "the score" in all matters of interpretation. We trust it will now be clear that these dicta were the simple offhand counsels of a real Artist to neophytes wishing help from the famous. But was this advice, in every detail and circumstance, really what the original composer would desire? Weighing this primal argument from Goerne and others that the score (*urtext* or edited) is the Mount Sinai of each composed musical work, the key question is "Should Goerne's words and other such pronouncements be taken to heart by aspiring artists; is creating great music really that simple?"

We do not believe so. Goerne and others represent the fully formed Artist, for whom an assumed, simple adherence to the score may indeed succeed, but because of a number of critical reasons. Some of these reasons are, in fact, at the very opposite extreme of simple score reliance: the accumulation of knowledge, for example, and the awareness of one's own inspired feelings, thoughts, and personality, all leading to a habitual pursuit of discoveries which are followed to their ultimate destiny.

The unavoidable fact is that the composer *needs* the aid and sincere contribution of the Artist's **interpretive** experience and judgment. Otherwise, since not every detail of a work-in-concept can be adequately notated, only the composer could perform it, within his/her own limitations and stipulations, with the result that performances would be confined to the composer's insights during the brief duration of his life.[1]

Thus: central here is the implication of trust—trust between composer and performer to share in creative and interpretive **Artistry,** trust between performer and audience to share in the serious communication of worthwhile literature.

There is also the matter of trust between students striving toward Artistry and the teachers who are seeking to guide them to it. If there were only one legitimate interpretation of every detail in a work, then the role of the teacher would be to simply deliver the work as a fixed "frozen image" for every student to copy. But to repeat: it is one of the refreshing strengths of music as an art form that much performance variety is possible—and welcome—without the abandonment of essential messages. As we have suggested, too many in the performance field are afraid or unwilling to experiment very much, believing their duty is to follow the score markings explicitly (naively assuming that the way in which they happen to discern these markings matches perfectly with what the composer had in mind). We have demonstrated that such is a faulted journey, because the composers'

---

1   This is the direction that—too often in recent decades—American popular music has taken. When the "artist" dies, much of her/his music dies too.

wishes are not completely known, and possibly of a changing nature, anyway.[2]

What are the Wellsprings of Taste?

How can one know to place one's trust in the taste of a given musician—composer or performer? Is taste (1) *Inborn?* (2) *Inbred?* (3) *Coached?* (4) *Instructed?* That is, is an individual (1) blessed at birth, with an otherwise inexplicable gift from God, (2) born with inherited good genes, (3) born gifted, but directed in certain performance aspects of certain works, or (4) taught mostly from scratch?

Put another way, can Artistry be developed, or is one hopelessly pigeon-holed by fate?

Today the fashionable exemplar is Mozart, Mozart, Mozart. Hopeful young parents rush out to buy stacks of Mozart CDs to run during Sweetum's time in the womb, naps, and crib-play, in hopes of enhancing the child's cortical development. And audiences celebrate "child prodigies", but then forget the very name of the prodigy when she/he turns out to be an unexceptional twenty-year-old. They come to prefer hearing an eighty-eight-year-old Rubinstein play two concerti on one *Concertgebouw* program. [EN 12-11]

---

2 While preparing to perform Aaron Copland's *Piano Sonata* in 1960, the renowned Byron Janis went to the composer's house to play it for him. "On arriving at his home, I found him tinkering with one of its passages and said, 'Mr. Copland, I notice you are playing *forte* and you have marked it *piano* in the score'. He turned to me grinning mischievously and said, 'Ah, but that was ten years ago'." [EN 12-9] Similarly, in a 1995 interview, the late American pianist John Browning recalled what the composer Samuel Barber once told him: "I never expect the artist who's playing my music to say: 'How do you want it'? What I'm interested in is what my music does with the artist. It's the catalyst. There is no *one* way." [EN 12-10]

Along with using one's talents and intuition to foster interpretation, it is necessary to work and study with diligence to build Artistry. Mozart himself acknowledged this in private correspondence: "People err who think my art comes easily to me. I assure you, dear friend, nobody has devoted so much time and thought to composition as I. There is not a famous master whose music I have not industriously studied through many times."

If we are to accept a current public view of Wolfgang Amadeus Mozart, he was the living example of our (1) above, the babe "born bearing an otherwise inexplicable gift from God" who could create wondrous music in his crib. But of course, this is hardly the whole story. The sometimes-overlooked fact is that his father, Leopold Mozart, was the greatest violin teacher of his day, and aggressively promoted his son as a "prodigy" from infancy; thus, the father obtained for the son *entrée* to the royal/imperial courts of the Habsburgs and the Bourbons. Young Wolfgang was tutored in writing for orchestra on a long visit in the London home of Johann Christophe Bach (youngest son of the great Sebastian Bach), studied counterpoint and other matters with the famed Padre Martini during a lengthy stay in Italy, and went on meeting and learning from the finest musicians in Europe who were his father's friends. He discovered the counterpoint of Sebastian Bach during a trip to Leipzig before writing the *finale* of his last symphony. He dedicated his six greatest string quartets to "Papa Haydn" after studying Haydn's own latest ones.

In short, even with little "*Wolferl*" it was nature *and* nurture. It is not established fact that one is simply "born with it." We should respect our own gifts, and trust our own intuition.

Then added study, practice, thought, and discipline can build an Artist.

Words and Music…Again

Since Chapter One we have confronted a sequence of issues that the authors believe often impede the development of Artistry, including: (1) exclusive and rigid focus on the score and **technique**; (2) confused terminology in communication; (3) insufficient attention to historical and biographical background; (4) misconceptions regarding the world of "prodigies;" and (5) failure to pursue music as a unique, non-verbal language.

In approaching musical language, one should part from verbal languages (save for the useful metaphor). In the novel *War and Peace*, Prince Andrew Bolkonski asks Natasha Rostov whether he "may hope" she will agree to be his wife: "He looked at her and was struck by the serious impassioned expression on her face. Her face said: 'Why ask? Why doubt what you cannot but know? Why speak, when words cannot express what one feels?'" EN 12-12

Just so, we must turn from words to music—the latter tantamount in every way to a separate equivalently-meaningful language—to express that of which verbiage often proves itself incapable.

We venture cautiously to address every reader, serious student, teacher, and professional concert performer. Each appearance offers the musician(s) involved the opportunity to literally bring a new artwork into the world, a composition never heard before. But first the performer must be committed, not to routine repetition, but to a personal Artistry that enables merging with the composer (and audience) in this new creation. And if we are to be Artists, we must free ourselves to interpret, considering carefully the era in which the composer lived, and finding a vision that goes far beyond the printed score.

We must believe that music is a whole, primary language.

The aural structures which we can envision, and which we can make palpable to our audiences, are virtual Parthenons—clumsily damaged at times in the past by human shallowness, but yet capable of drawing gasps of admiration from those who today perceive them. And now it is given to us to restore them. As Artists, we have wide latitude and a moral responsibility.

We must fully enrich our audiences. We are the curators, and in our hands are—not those Parthenons—but Bach, Beethoven, Brahms, and all the great ones.

APPENDIX:
Expanding the Base

Bernhard Heiden, protégé of Paul Hindemith and former chair of the composition department at Indiana University, once told author Demaree that the very first time he heard Béla Bartók's *Concerto for Orchestra* (1943) he "knew it was a masterpiece". As the twenty-first century continues to unfold, we look forward with hope to the creation of new music masterpieces, recognizing that these will likely come from a broader geographical and population base than previously. For this reason, it is encouraging that composers from a wider swath of the world's countries and origins are currently being recognized and performed globally. Prejudices that made advancement difficult for outstanding talents like Fanny Mendelssohn, Clara Schumann and unknown numbers of racially diverse composers, are falling away. In the field of music performance, we currently enjoy the artistry of multitudes of musicians from formerly dismissed and disadvantaged classes, who are now welcomed and flourish with prominence. Among the endless examples is noted conductor Gustavo Dudamel, who along with other impressive musicians emerged from **El Sistema** in Venezuela—a music education program for the poor which has had a profound impact since its founding in 1975. It is to our great benefit that a similar receptivity is expanding in the field of composition. The world of music cannot afford to ignore or waste any of its precious resources.

Glossary

These Technical Terms
(Limited Herein as Follows)
Recast in **Bold o**n Their First Appearance in Each Chapter

artistry, artistic

a maturity of music performance which enlivens and enriches notated work; performance(s) characteristic of that maturity

expressivity

the capability to make clarifying and/or enriching interpretive choices, unique to an individual performer—choices which may add variety and/or "personality" to an interpretation; may be understood as "clarifying the given musical context"

intuition, intuitive

insight or interpretive skill apparent in an Artist's performance; personal to that performer, and not to the influences of teachers or others; uniquely interpretive

interpretation, interpretive

a process of expressing in a more-or-less unique fashion passages of music, whether (a) done under the influence of other performers or scholars, or (b) done out of personal insights into the character/history of the music

musical, musicality	WORDS TO AVOID; technical terms made misleading or harmful by casual overuse; unteachable
phrasing	A TERM MADE CONFUSING BY MULTIPLE USAGES; especially (1) for analysts of scores usually a series of cadential decisions; (2) for many vocal and instrumental performers a matter of decisions about where the "line" should "breathe" (irrespective of cadence locations)
pliability	manipulation of rhythm, counterpoint, *tempi,* and/or dynamics, etc., any or all of which may allow an Artist to perform personally and more-or-less uniquely; malleability; freedom of interpretation
rigidity, rigid	inflexibility of rhythm, especially in forcing

spiral study, the	evolving, comprehensive system of preparation for performance of a given work or a related body of works
style, stylistic	an established realm of interpretive and expressive choices; an agreed or shared set of interpretive limits for works sharing certain characteristics
talent, talented	WORDS TO AVOID; having recognized and/or latent insights or skills; as technical terms these words are made misleading and/or harmful by casual overuse; unteachable
taste, tastefulness	sharing the expressive or interpretive views current among others present at the moment, irrespective of the supposed intentions of the composer, or others; being "in fashion"
technique	clusters of basic neuro-muscular skills necessary to the most elementary levels of performance (*i.e., fingerings, tonguing, etc.*) dependent on phys-

ical development; generally the first stage in studio work (performance studies)

tradition
an inherited, often more-or-less rigid approach to the interpretation of a given score, composer, or "school"

Bibliography

Adler *School*
Adler, Guido, "Haydn and the Viennese Classical School," *The Musical Quarterly 18:191-207 April 1932*

Anderson *Europe*
Anderson, Matthew S., *Europe in the Eighteenth Century; 1713-1783,* New York, Holt, Rinehart, and Winston, 1961

Bach *Versuch*
Bach, Carl Philipp Emanuel, *Versuch über die wahre Art das Clavier zu spielen:* see Mitchell *Versuch*

Bacon *Notes*
Bacon, Ernst, *Notes on the Piano,* Syracuse, Syracuse Univ. Press, 1963

Bartók *NYT Obituary I*
Obituary for Bartók, Bela, in *New York Times,* 09/27/1945

Bartók *NYT Reburial II*
"Obituary for Bartók's Budapest Reburial", in *New York Times,* 07/08/1988

Barton *RSC*
Barton, John, master class writer and presenter, *Playing Shakespeare,*

DVD in 4 vols, produced and distributed by Athena, ITV Global Entertainment, and Acorn Media Group, 1984

Bernstein *Secrets*   Bernstein, J. quoting Lord John Maynard Keynes, in his essay "The Secrets of the Old One, Part II", *The New Yorker*, March 17, 1973

Bertenssohn *Rachmaninoff*   Bertensson, Sergei, *Sergei Rachmaninoff: A Lifetime in Music,* New York, NY Univ. Press, 1956

Brown *Chopin*   Brown, Maurice J.E., *Chopin, Fryderyk Fanciszek, Work List,* in *New Grove Dictionary of Music and Musicians, Thr.* ed. by Stanley Sadie in 20 vols., London, Macmillan Publishers, Ltd, 1980, vol. 4, 307-308

Chasins *Pianists*   Chasins, Abram, *Speaking of Pianists...,* New York, Alfred A. Knopf, 1958

Christ *Structure*   Christ, William B. et al., *Materials and Structures of Music*, two vols., Prentice-Hall, Englewood Cliffs, NJ, 1967

Churchill *Storm*

Churchill, Winston S., *The Gathering Storm*, vol. 1 of 6 of *The Second World War*, Boston, MA, Houghton Mifflin Co., 1948

Cone *Form*

Cone, Edward T., *Musical Form and Musical Performance*, New York, W.W. Norton & Co., Inc. 1968

Demaree *Bach Invocation*

Demaree, Robert W., Jr., *Leipzig 1735*, excerpt from printed concert program, South Bend, IN, Indiana Univ. South Bend, 1985, opening

Demaree *Haydn Quartets*

–*Structural Proportions of the Haydn Quartets, The*, diss., Bloomington, IN, Indiana University, 1973, Ann Arbor, MI, University Microfilms Inc.

Demaree/Moses *Complete*

Demaree, Robert W., Jr. and Don V Moses, *Complete Conductor, The; A Comprehensive Resource for the Professional Conductor*, Bloomington. IN, Indiana University Press, 1995

Demaree/Moses *HM*   Demaree, Robert W., and Don
                          V Moses, *The Masses of Joseph
                          Haydn. History, Style, Perfor-
                          mance,* Rochester Hills, MI, Clas-
                          sical Heritage, 2008

Dies *Haydn*   Dies, Albert Christoph, *Biogra-
                          phische Nachrichten von Joseph
                          Haydn,* transl. in Gotwals, Ver-
                          non, *Haydn, Two Contemporary
                          Portraits,* Madison, WI, Univ of
                          Wisconsin Press, 1968

Doidge *Brain*   Doidge, Norman, MD, *The Brain
                          That Changes Itself,* NY, Viking,
                          Penguin Group, 2007, Emphasis
                          on Neuroplasticity

Drake *Beethoven*   Drake, Kenneth, *The Sonatas of
                          Beethoven as he played and taught
                          them,* Cincinnati, Music Teachers
                          National Assoc., Inc., 1972

Duffie *Broadcast*   Duffie, Bruce, Broadcast inter-
                          view with Browning, recorded
                          October 13, 1995 for WNIB Ra-
                          dio, Chicago

Eagleman *Brain*   Eagleman, David, *The Brain*, NY, Pantheon Books (Penguin Random House), 2015

Gardner *Bach*   Gardiner, John Eliot, *Bach, Music in the Castle of Heaven*, New York, Alfred A. Knopf, 2013

Gates-Coon *Princes*   Gates-Coon, Rebecca, *The Landed Estates of the Esterhazy Princes*, Baltimore, John Hopkins Univ. Press, 1994

Geiringer *Haydn*   Geiringer, Karl, *Haydn, A Creative Life in Music,* with Irene Geiringer, Berkeley and Los Angeles, Univ of California Press, 1968

Gotwals *Genius*   Gotwals, Vernon, *Joseph Haydn, Eighteenth-Century Gentleman and Genius,* Univ. of Wisconsin Press, Madison, WI, 1963. This incorporates Gotwals' own transl. *(*see listings herein) of both Dies, *Biographische Nachrichten von Joseph Haydn* and Griesinger, *Biographische Notizen über Joseph Haydn*

Graf *Legend*   Graf, Max, *Legend of a Musical City*, Greenwood Press, New York,

| | Copyright 1945 by Philosophical Library, Inc., Reprinted with permission of Philosophical Library, Inc. by Greenwood Reprinting, 1969 |

Griesinger *Haydn* — Griesinger, George A, *Biographische Notizen über Joseph Haydn*, transl. in Gotwals, Vernon, *Haydn, Two Contemporary Portraits*, Madison, WI, Univ of Wisconsin Press, 1967

Hallé *Life/Letters* — Hallé, C.E. and Marie, *Life and Letters of Sir Charles Hallé*, London, Smith & Elder, 1896

Herford *Obituary* — Herford, Julius, Obituary (author unknown), NY, *New York Times*, 09/18/1981

Hickok *Rachmaninoff* — Hickok, Lorena A., Rachmaninoff Interview, *Minneapolis Tribune*, November 11, 1921.

Hotz *Brain* — Hotz, Robert Lee, "Research Shows Brain Works as Word Cloud", news report, *Wall Street Journal*, 04/28/2016, p. A7

Hotz *Judge*

"Art--Is It Beautiful? How Our Brains Judge Art in Seconds", news report, *Wall Street Journal*, 12/08/2015, pp. D1-3

Hudson *Chaconne*

Hudson, Richard, "Chaconne" in *New Grove Dictionary of Music and Musicians, Thr.* ed. by Stanley Sadie in 20 vols., London, Macmillan Publishers, Ltd., 1980, vol. 4, p. 102

Isacoff *Temperament*

Isacoff, Stuart, *Temperament, How Music Became a Battleground for the Great Minds of Western* Civilization, New York, Vintage Books, Random House, Inc., 2003

Janis *Infidelity*

Janis, Byron, essay "In Praise of Infidelity," *Wall Street Journal*, 01/06/2010, p. B13

Jenkins *Everest*

Jenkins, Mark, "Maxed Out On Everest," *Official Journal of the National Geographic Society*, June 2013

Keller *Articulation*

Keller, Hermann, *Phrasing and Articulation,* transl. by Leigh Gerdine, New York, W. W. Norton & Co., 1965

Kelly *Reminiscences*

Kelly, Michael, *Reminiscences of Michael Kelly of the King's Theatre, and Theatre Royal, Drury Lane,* in 2 vols., transcr. by Theodore Hook, London, Henry Colborn, 1826

Kerman/Tyson *Beethoven*

Kerman, Joseph, and Alan Tyson, "Beethoven, Ludwig van," in *New Grove Dictionary of Music and Musicians, Thr.* ed. by Stanley Sadie in 20 vols., London, Macmillan Publishers, Ltd., 1980, vol. 12, p. 354

Kirby *Keyboard*

Kirby, F. E., *A Short History of Keyboard Music,* New York, The Free Press, 1966

Knocker/L Mozart *Violinschule*

Knocker, Editha, *A Treatise on the Fundamental Principles of Violin Playing,* 2nd ed., London, Oxford Univ. Press, 1951; transl. of Leopold Mozart's *Versuch einer grunclichen Violinschule,* Augsburg, 1756

Kurzweil *Mind*

Kurzweil, Ray, *How To Create A Mind,* NY, Penguin Books, 2012

Lampert/Somfai *Bartók*   Lampert, Vera, and Laszlo Somfai, "Bartók, Bela," in *New Grove Dictionary of Music and Musicians, Thr.* ed. by Stanley Sadie in 20 vols., London, Macmillan Publishers, Ltd., 1980, vol. 2, pp. 197-225

Langer *Feeling*   Langer, Suzanne K., *Feeling and Form,* New York, Charles Scribner's Sons, 1953

Langer *Philosophy*   ---*Philosophy in a New Key,* Cambridge, MA., Harvard Univ. Press, 1957

Larsen *Viennese*   Larsen, Jens Peter, *Handel, Haydn, and the Viennese Classical Style,* Ann Arbor, UMI Research Press, 1981

Lendvai *Hungarians*   Lendvai, Paul, trans. by Ann Major, *The Hungarians, A Thousand Years of Victory in Defeat,* Princeton, N.J., Princeton University Press, 1999

Levitin *Brain*   Levitin, Daniel J., *This is Your Brain on Music, The Science of a Human Obsession,* NY, Plume Book, Penguin Group, 2007

Luey *Child*   Luey, Beth, and Saperstein, Stella,
                                *The Harmonious Child, Every Par-
                                ent's Guide to Musical Instruments,
                                Teachers, and Lessons,* Berkeley/To-
                                ronto, Celestial Arts, 2003

Meyer *Emotion*   Meyer, Leonard, *Emotion and
                                Meaning in Music,* Chicago, Univ
                                of Chicago Press, 2nd impres, 1957

Machlis *Enjoyment*   Machlis, Joseph, *The Enjoyment of
                                Music,* New York, 1955

Mersmann *Mozart*   Mersmann, Hans, ed., *Letters of
                                Wolfgang Amadeus Mozart,* trans.
                                by M.M. Bozman for USA reissue
                                by Dover Publications, 2016

Miller *Nielsen*   Miller, Mina (ed.), *The Nielsen
                                Companion,* Portland, OR, Ama-
                                deus Press, 1995

Mitchell *Versuch*   Mitchell, William J., transl. with
                                Felix Salzer the Carl Friedrich
                                Emanuel Bach, *Versuch über die
                                wahre Art das Clavier zu spielen,* as
                                *The True Art of Playing Keyboard
                                Instruments,* New York, 1949.

Moses/Demaree/Ohmes
Face to Face

Moses, Don V, Robert W. Demaree, Jr., and Allen F. Ohmes, *Face to Face with Orchestra and Chorus, A Handbook for Choral Conductors,* 2nd (expanded) ed., Indiana University Press, Bloomington, IN, 2004

Newman *Bach*

Newman, Anthony, *Bach and the Baroque,* 2nd ed., Stuyvesant, New York, Pendragon Press, 1995

Pinker *Mind*

Pinker, Steven, *How The Mind Works,* NY, W.W. Norton & Co., Inc., reissued 2009

Pohl *Haydn*

Pohl, Karl Ferdinand, *Joseph Haydn,* Berlin, 1875-1927, Breitkopf und Härtel, in 3 vols., Vol. I (to 1766), Vol. II (to 1790), Vol. III completed by Hugo Botstiber; reprinted in Weisbaden by Sändig, 1970-1971

Ratner *Eighteenth-Century*

Ratner, Leonard G., "Eighteenth-Century Theories of Musical Period Structure", *The Musical Quarterly* 42:439-454, October 1956

Ratner *Harmonic*

—"Harmonic Aspects of Classic Form", *Journal of the American Musicological Society* 2:159-168, Fall 1949

Richardson *Metronome*

Richardson, E.G., "Metronome," in *New Grove Dictionary of Music and Musicians, Thr,* ed. by Stanley Sadie in 20 vols., London, Macmillan Publishers, Ltd., 1980, vol. 12, p. 223

Rubinstein *Broadcast*

Rubinstein, Artur, (Interview by Harry Reasoner for CBS Reports during Royal Concergebouw Orchestra recorded Concert), Amsterdam

Sadie *Mozart*

Sadie, Stanley, "Mozart, Wolfgang Amadeus", in *New Grove Dictionary of Music and Musicians, Thr,* ed. by Stanley Sadie in 20 vols., London, Macmillan Publishers, Ltd., 1980, vol. 12, p. 687

Salzer *Structural*

Salzer, Felix, *Structural Hearing,* 2 vols, Charles Boni, NY, 1952

Samson *Chopin*

Samson, Jim, *Chopin, The Four Ballades,* Cambridge Music Handbooks, Cambridge University Press, Cambridge, UK, 1992

Schousboe *Nielsen*

Schousboe, Torben, "Nielsen, Carl" in *New Grove Dictionary of Music and Musicians, Thr,* ed. by Stanley Sadie in 20 vols., London, Macmillan Publishers, Ltd., 1980, vol. 13, pp. 225-230

Shakespeare *Hamlet*

Shakespeare, William, *The Tragedy of Hamlet, Prince of Denmark* in The Heritage Shakespeare: The Tragedies, NY, The Heritage Press, 1958

Simpson *Nielsen*

Simpson, Robert, *Carl Nielsen: Symphonist,* Taplinger Publishing Co., Inc., NY, 1979

Slominsky *Bartók*

Slominsky, Nicolas, "Bartók, Béla", in *Baker's Biographical Dictionary of Musicians, Sixth Edition,* NY, Schirmer Books, 1978, p. 107

Slominsky *Broadwood*

"Broadwood & Sons" in *Baker's Biographical dictionary of Musicians, Sixth Edition,* NY, Schirmer Books, 1978, p. 235

Slominsky *Maelzel*

"Metronome", in *Baker's Biographical Dictionary of Musicians, Sixth Edition*, NY, Schirmer Books, 1978, p. 223

Stevens *Bartók*

Stevens, Halsey, *The Life and Music of Bela Bartók,* rev. edit., Oxford Univ. Press, New York, 1964

Strasser *bezahltt*

Strasser, Otto, *Und dafür wird man noch bezahlt, ein Leben mit den Wiener Phiharmoniker,* München, Deutwcher Taschenbuch Verlag, 1984

Stravinsky *Poetics*

Stravinsky, Igor, *Poetics of Music in the Form of Six Lessons*, transl. by Arthur Knodel and Ingolf Dahl, *Preface by Darius Milhaud,* New York, Vintage Books, 1956

Swafford *Brahms*

Swafford, Jan, *Johannes Brahms, a Biography,* Vintage Books, Random House. Inc. New York, 1995

Teachout *Trick*

Teachout, Terry, "The Trick of Translation," essay in *The Wall Street Journal*, 08/16/2013, p. D7

Tolstoy *Maude*   Tolstoy, Leo (Lev), *War and Peace,* transl. by Louise and Aylmer Maude for Oxford Univ. Press, NY, Simon and Schuster, 1942

Vignal *Haydn*   Vignal, Marc, *Franz Joseph Haydn,* transl. by author Demaree, Paris, Editions Seghers, 1963

Westrup *Conducting*   Westrup, Jack, "Conducting," in *New Grove Dictionary of Music and Musicians, Thr,* ed. by Stanley Sadie in 20 vols., London, Macmillan Publishers Ltd., 1980, vol. 4, pp.643-645.

Endnotes Chapter One

1-1 See for example Beethoven's sketch for the Piano Sonata in E Major, Opus 109 Artaria 195, transcribed, edited and with commentary by William Kinderman, University of Illinois Press, 2003.

1-2 See scores of his *Rumanian Folk Dances (1915), Mikrokosmos (1926-39),* and *Piano Sonata (1926).*

1-3 See detailed audience reports quoted in Chapter Three, p. 35, and Chapter Eleven, pp. 166-7

1-4 Shakespeare *Hamlet, Act III, Scene 4*

1-5 Much attention has been drawn in recent years to the startling accumulation of clutter left behind by self-possessed climbers attempting to "conquer" Mt. Everest, leaving behind in the frozen upper stages (above 27,000 feet) of the iconic mountain mummified corpses, excrement, food containers, shelters, discarded oxygen tanks, and literally tons of general trash. Among the most detailed accounts is the essay q.v. Jenkins *Everest.*

1-6 One recalls a television performer who claimed popular credit for playing Chopin's "Minute Waltz" in less than sixty seconds, apparently unaware himself that the word "Minute" in the *French* title actually referred to the unusual brevity of the work.

1-7 Machlis, *p. 217*

1-8 Prominent examples include the first movement of Prokofiev's *Sixth Sonata, op. 82,* the fourth movement of the Barber
Sonata, op. 26, the finale of the Saint-Saens *Piano concerto No.
2, op. 22,* and the Tchaikovsky *First Piano Concerto, op. 23.*

1-9 Westrup. (See the summary of conducting history.) Especially with *concerti,* of course, the modern responsibilities of
the conductor to (1) "beat time" and (2) "interpret" (the composer's wishes) become sometimes confused.

1-10 Author Demaree, visiting then in Austria, recalls with
some embarrassment having listened to an ÖRF (Österreich-
sher Rundfunk) interview of Leonard Bernstein as he explained
pridefully how he had just lectured the assembled members of
the <u>Wiener Philharmoniker,</u> no less, on the nature and performance of *their* famous "uneven waltz beat." (Bernstein, however, as conductor/author Don V Moses has observed, could be
a master of rehearsal management.)

1-11 On tour, Constitution Hall, Washington, DC, November 1958; afternoon rehearsal and evening public performance.
Some members of the evening audience may have loved his
"pleading genuflections", but Demaree could *hear* no difference. He still regards Ormandy's behaviors as condescending
to the ticket-buyers, who seemed not to notice that the players
weren't watching the conductor closely anyway.

Endnotes Chapter Two

2-1 Robert Shaw: conversation with author Demaree and Don V Moses, Cleveland, OH, March 1987.

2-2 Pivotal line from the script of the 1967 Warner Bros. film *Cool Hand Luke;* screenplay by Dean Pearce. Originally spoken by actor Strother Martin.

2-3 See the discussion of Tuning and Temperament in Chapter Seven, p. 94. These mechanisms *do not* affect meaning.

2-4 Even between two *verbal* languages one can find occasional cognates: as was said about a friend of one of the authors, "She's just lucky that in Germany they pronounce 'Beer' ('Bier') the same way!"

2-5 See discussion on pp. 169-70

2-6 Similarly, some public schools have included a grade for "citizenship" on student evaluations, and that word could be defined by the individual teacher to mean whatever she or he wished to reward or punish.

2-7 They are listed in the Glossary, among the terms which are technically defined there for use herein. Other terms can be construed carefully in their places.

2-8 Beethoven himself began a passage in his *Choral Fantasia, op. 80,* with the instruction *"Allegretto ma non troppo quasi Andante con moto".* (See Moses, Demaree, and Ohmes, *Face to Face with Orchestra and Chorus,* p.187.) In the 1930's some Viennese folk joked that Webern was now using a symbol he called *pensato,* which demanded *a dynamic level so soft it could only be "thought."* Conversation with the late Otto Strasser and author Demaree, Eisenstadt, Austria, August 1968.

Endnotes Part II

II-1 John Barton, co-founder of the Royal Shakespeare Company, in introducing *Playing Shakespeare*, a series of workshops recorded in 1982 by British Television.

II-2 Pianist-writer-broadcaster Paul Harvey, Jr., in conversation with present author Hamilton, 2014.

II-3 David Mermelstein *Follow the Lieder, a Cultural Conversation with Matthias Goerne,* Wall Street Journal, April 16, 2012.

II-4 In courses especially at Indiana University Bloomington in the 1960's and on through the end of his career (in that era before laptops existed), from literally dozens of very closely-written legal pads, one heard Herford lecture on composers from Josquin and Palestrina to Monteverdi, Beethoven, Brahms, and Britten. For *Spiral Study,* see the Glossary.

Endnotes Chapter Three

3-1 Pianist-writer-broadcaster Paul Harvey, Jr., in conversation with present author Hamilton, 2010.

3-2 There is—and probably always will be—continuing and deleterious confusion about opus numbers in the works of Chopin. This *Polonaise-fantaisie* is a painful example: it is commonly known as "op.61," *and even thus identified by Jim Samson* (Samson *Chopin*, pp. 3, 21, and 88), but is actually no.159 in the chronological listing by J. E. Brown in the *New Grove* "Chopin" (NG4:307-308)—thus one of the very last of his compositions. Some of this disorder no doubt arises from the early successes of his "patriotic Polish works," juxtaposed against the delayed public enthusiasm for his later, more mature works.

3-3 It is in ternary form—which predominates everywhere in this period—but is handled freely.

3-4 See Janis *Infidelity,* p. 195

Endnotes Chapter Four

4-1 Slonimsky *Broadwood*, p.351

4-2 Slonimsky *Maetzel*, p.1068

4-3 Richardson, p.223

4-4 Kerman/Tyson, p.354

4-5 Kerman/Tyson

Endnotes Chapter Five

5-1 Demaree/Moses *HM,* pp. 30ff, 775-778

5-2 Charles VI, Fux, and Vivaldi. *ibid,* p.9

5-3 And after he was taken to play for the Queen of France, he was said to have exclaimed petulantly "Who is this lady who does not kiss me? The Empress kissed me!"

5-4 Mozart, *Violinschule.* SEE Knocker, *Violinschule.*

5-5 ...and of his host, J.C. Bach, as well as his father. (Note, among other suspicious scholars, the use of the word "purportedly" in the detailed article in Slonimsky, *Mozart,* p.1597.) The two Mozarts' stay there on Ebury Street is commemorated on a local plaque at the site, two-and-a-half centuries later.

5-6 See our discussions of "child prodigies" in Chapter Eight, pp. 103-6, and of Mozart as an exemplar in Chapter Twelve, pp. 179-81.

5-7 The following pages (approximately to the death of Mozart) are drawn largely from the opening chapters of Demaree and Moses *The Masses of Joseph Haydn* [Demaree/Moses *HM*] and the research is current (2008).

5-8 It is the view of Demaree/Moses that Haydn's role was to become "The Architect of the Classical Style."

5-9 op cit., p.83

5-10 Larsen, p.117

5-11 op cit., p.147; Geiringer p, 64

5-12 Vignal *Stravinsky*, cited in Demaree *Haydn Quartets*, p.X

5-13 Demaree/Moses *HM*, pp.30-31

5-14 *ibid.*

5-15 Geiringer p. 83

5-16 *ibid.*

Endnotes Chapter Six

6-1 Hamburg, Bremen, and Lubeck were the last active members of *Hanse SWAFFORD* when that decrepit organization at last formally disbanded in the mid-nineteenth century. As of this writing, Hamburg remains the second-largest city in reunified Germany.

6-2 The Reeperbahn is the core of Hamburg's notorious St. Pauli "entertainment" district.

6-3 Swafford pp. 1-15

6-4 *ibid.* pp. 28-31

6-5 The famous, disastrous debut of his first piano concerto in Leipzig was counteracted over the remainder of his life by frequent performances of his works at the *Gewandhaus*. See Young "Leipzig", NG 10:639.

6-6 Swafford, p. 217

6-7 Graf, p. 103

6-8 *ibid.* pp 98-100

6-9 Swafford, p 606

6-10 *ibid.* p. 612

6-11 *ibid.* pp. 632-633

Endnotes Chapter Seven

7-1 Demaree *Bach Invocation.* These opening paragraphs are drawn from a 1985 concert program, *Leipzig 1735...*, celebrating *in der deutschen Sprache* the 300th birthday of J.S.Bach. (It was a replication of all the components of an Easter service at Thomaskirche under Bach's hand in that year.)

7-2 But as late as the 1934 *Mathis der Maler* and the 1940 *The Four Temperaments,* Hindemith continued to seek to put his tuning and tonal theories into practice. And see Isacoff, pp. 216-218.

7-3 Henceforward "WTC"

7-4 And perhaps other (lost) *Passions...*

Endnotes Chapter Eight

8-1 The interviewer was Harry Reasoner.

8-2 M/D/O *Face to Face*, p.168

8-3 See the one on p. 105

8-4 A century later the Nazis were not fooled!

8-5 See Chapter Three.

8-6 A remarkably modern view! Herein see the "clouds" section of Chapter Twelve, pp. 173-4. And see particularly the cogent and compelling analysis of this important issue in Gardiner, pp. 434 ff.

Endnotes Chapter Nine

9-1 Swafford, p. 524

9-2 Hudson "Chaconne", NG p. 103

9-3 At the moment his principal biography appears to be by Torben Schousboe at NG13:225-230. If his later symphonies (and works ranking with the *Chaconne, op.32*) gain attention, however, other scholarship may deservedly emerge. See below the Simpson assessments of those later symphonies, for example.

9-4 *ibid.*

9-5 *ibid.*

9-6 *ibid.*

9-7 *ibid.*

9-8 Simpson, p. 164

Endnotes Chapter Ten

10-1 Lendvai, pp.10-11

10-2 Churchill, vol. 1, p. 10.

10-3 Stevens, p. 93

10-4 *ibid.*

10-5 *ibid.*, pp.92-93

10-6 *ibid.*

10-7 Composer (and Hindemith protege´) Bernhard Heiden once in author Demaree's presence said of the work that the Bartók *Concerto for Orchestra* was the "only Twentieth Century work he knew on one hearing to be a masterpiece!"

10-8 Part of his fury may have emerged from his realization that his Hungarian birthplace had now become Romanian. (NG2:197.) Bartók's (and Churchill's) "Greater Hungary" was drawn and quartered in the Treaty of Versailles. See Churchill's historic outrage just above. *loc.cit.*, p. 135

10-9 See especially NG2:199 ff.

10-10 *ibid.*

10-11 Bartók NYT *Obituary I*

10-12 Bartók NYT *Reburial II*

Endnotes Part III

III-1 Chasins, p.41

III-2 Teachout, D7

Endnotes Chapter Eleven

11-1 See Chapter One, p. 13

11-2 Bertensson, p.195

11-3 Janis, p.B13

11-4 Drake, p.56 (italics added)

11-5 Bacon, p.8

11-6 *ibid.*, p.16

11-7 Chasins, p.44

11-8 Bacon, p.62

11-9 Newman, p.5

11-10 *ibid.*, p.250

11-11 Schonberg, p.25

11-12 *ibid.*, p.41

11-13 Drake, p.24

11-14 *op.cit.* Schonberg, p.79

11-15 *op.cit.* Drake, p.54

11-16 *op.cit.* Schonberg, pp.84-86

11-17 *ibid.*

11-18 *op.cit.* Drake, p.45

11-19 *ibid*, pp.23-24

11-20 *op.cit.* Schonberg, p.132

11-21 *ibid.*, p.28

11-22 *ibid.*, pp.125-126

11-23 Hallé, p.36

11-24 *op.cit.* Schonberg, p.167

11-25 *ibid.*, p.130

11-26 *ibid.*, p.125

11-27 *ibid.*, p.132

Endnotes Chapter Twelve

12-1 See Part II, p. 26

12-2 Similarly, consider the possible range of unsought connections for: "Babe Ruth", or "To be, or not to be," or "Lili Marlene'," or "Berlin,", or "Titanic."

12-3 There are many research books in Cognitive Science published over the past two decades, but this field of study is especially active and ongoing, and has grown more so in the last dozen years or so. Consult the Bibliography.

12-4 Hotz Judge

12-5 Shakespeare *Hamlet,* Act 3, Scene 4

12-6 See Chapter Nine, pp. 128-9

12-7 See Chapter One, p. 4

12-8 See Part II, p. 25

12-9 Janis, p. B13

12-10 Duffle Broadcast

12-11 Rubinstein, Broadcast. In his last years, Artur Rubinstein recorded a Concertgebouw concert on which he performed both of the Brahms piano concertos as part of a *CBS Reports* broadcast. (During a putative "intermission" interview with Harry Reasoner in his dressing room, he remarked that he was "the luckiest of men, because all my life I have loved music.")

12-12 Tolstoy, p.525